Help!

I've Been Asked to Preach

Sinking

Don't Panic... Here's Practical Help to Keep Your Sermon From

Maylan Schurch

Autumn House® Publishing

www.autumnhousepublishing.com

A Division of **REVIEW AND HERALD®** PUBLISHING

Since 1861

Copyright © 2007 by
Review and Herald® Publishing Association

Published by Autumn House® Publishing, a division of Review and Herald® Publishing, Hagerstown, MD 21741-1119

Autumn House® titles may be purchased in bulk for educational, business, fund-raising, or sales promotional use. For information, please e-mail SpecialMarkets@reviewandherald.com.

Autumn House® Publishing publishes biblically based materials for spiritual, physical, and mental growth and Christian discipleship.

The author assumes full responsibility for the accuracy of all facts and quotations as cited in this book.

Unless otherwise indicated, texts are from the New King James Version. Copyright © 1979, 1980, 1982 by Thomas Nelson, Inc. Used by permission. All rights reserved.

Texts credited to Message are from *The Message.* Copyright © 1993, 1994, 1995, 1996, 2000, 2001, 2002. Used by permission of NavPress Publishing Group.

Scriptures credited to NCV are quoted from *The Holy Bible, New Century Version,* copyright © 1987, 1988, 1991 by Word Publishing, Dallas, Texas 75039. Used by permission.

Texts credited to NIV are from the *Holy Bible, New International Version.* Copyright © 1973, 1978, 1984, International Bible Society. Used by permission of Zondervan Bible Publishers.

This book was
Edited by Gerald Wheeler
Copyedited by James Cavil
Cover design by Ron Pride
Interior design by Candy Harvey
Electronic makeup by Shirley M. Bolivar
Typeset: 11/14 Bembo

PRINTED IN U.S.A.

11 10 09 08 07   5 4 3 2 1

Library of Congress Cataloging-in-Publication Data

Schurch, Maylan.
  Help! I've been asked to preach : don't panic . . . here's practical help to keep your sermon fron sinking / Maylan Schurch.
      p. cm.
  Includes bibliographical references.
  ISBN-13: 978-0-8127-0430-3
  1. Preaching.   I. Title.
  BV4211.3.S38 2006
  251—dc22
                              2006035113

Dedication

Shelley, this book is for you—because if, over the years, you hadn't guided your beginner pastor-husband so lovingly yet persistently, he could never have written it. And maybe he wouldn't still be preaching.

Thank you for your wholehearted, people-sensitive partnership in our ministry—and for your love.

Books by Maylan Schurch

Justin Case Adventures:
   1. *The Case of the Stolen Red Mary*
   2. *The Desert Temple Mystery*
   3. *Danger Signals in Belize*
   4. *Trouble in Masai Mara*

Beware of the Crystal Dragon
Blinded by the Light
The Great Graffiti Mystery
The Rapture
Rescue From Beyond Orion
A Thousand Shall Fall
Under the Shadow

To order, **call 1-800-765-6955.**

Visit us at **www.reviewandherald.com** for information on other Review and Herald® products.

Acknowledgments

If you end up appreciating this book, there's a good chance you have the following people to thank. They read through the manuscript and told me what they liked—and they gave gracious feedback about what needed tweaking.

Thanks to lay preachers Richard Hammen, Keith Locke, Willman Rojas, Gene Trent (who not only commented on the manuscript but also introduced me to the MindManager outlining software, without which this book would have remained a distant gleam), Shelley Schurch, and Gayle Woodruff, for reading it from the perspective of actually having stood behind pulpits and preached real sermons.

Thanks to Marian Forschler for a detailed, multilevel read-through from a writer's perspective. Thanks to Kathy Locke for perceptive comments. Thanks to Sharon Miller for her suggestion about starting a sermon with a story and "leaving them hanging" about the outcome until the sermon's end; to Ann Gimbel and Gayle Woodruff for suggestions about the title; to Melanie Felton for helpful and focusing comments; and to Martha Hammen and Elsa Rojas and Kim Trent.

Thanks to pastor and ministerial director Bruce Koch for casting his experienced eye upon this material. Thanks to Pastors Ron Preast and Chester Schurch for carving time from their busy pastorates to give this book careful scrutiny and expert suggestions.

Thanks to Russell Anderson and George Pierson, two elders and lay preachers who somehow believed that the 19-year-old Maylan Schurch could prepare and preach lay sermons, and who wouldn't let him rest until he did.

Multiplied thanksgiving to book acquisitions editor Jeannette Johnson, whose clear vision and "you can do it" attitude has been helping jump-start my writing since the late 1980s. And it gives me great comfort to have had Gerald Wheeler's judicious, experienced editorial hand hovering over these pages.

And thanks to the Lord, who would not let me rest until I changed from college teaching (which I loved) to pastoring (which I also love), after having first provided me with a wife who loves pastoral ministry as much as I do.

Contents

A Letter to Pastors
who may be reading this

Dear Pastor:

If you're like me, your greatest joy (next to seeing a soul come to the Lord) is watching fire ignite in your members' eyes as they discover areas of service that exactly match their gifts. Maybe the reason you're glancing through this book is that you'd like to enhance the gift of lay preaching you see in some of your people.

My own lay preaching experiences provided part of the foundation for my ministry, and perhaps it was the same for you. However, at age 19, when first asked to preach, I had to pull my sermons together by trial and error. And I made the usual beginners' mistakes, simply because nobody gave me instructions. So on my own I did my best to create one topical sermon after another, because topical was all I knew.

During my early 30s I left another career to become a full-time pastor. I had just started seminary when someone introduced me to Charles W. Koller's book *Expository Preaching Without Notes*. I was intrigued—not so much about the "without notes" part as about the idea of expository preaching. Since then, probably 95 percent of my sermons have been expository, drawing my message from a single Bible chapter or significantly long passage.

Occasionally I've preached in other styles—topical, textual, narrative, even dramatic monologue—and all are excellent ways to deliver God's Word. But I still feel that because of creeping biblical illiteracy, and increasingly squishy Bible interpretation practices, a congregation needs a good basic diet of expository preaching. That's why, by actual count, I've created 617 brand-new, straight-from-scratch expository sermons during my pastoral ministry—and after this weekend it'll be 618. And by the time you're actually reading this, it'll be 30 or 40 more.

In addition, I've had the joy of conducting a few preaching workshops and watching laypersons try their hands at the expository method. I wrote this book to try to communicate the excitement I've felt—as lay preacher turned pastor—of really delving into a Bible passage and interpreting some of the truth within it.

I've designed this book both as a stand-alone guide and one that can also be used to mentor laypersons, either individually or in study groups. I hope it can both help them prepare expository sermons and avoid a lot of the discouragement that beginners sometimes feel.

If you'd like, you can use it in a three-month small group setting. I've arranged the material into 12 chapters, with Group Discussion Starters (through chapter 10) as well as homework assignments.

My prayer is that the Holy Spirit will use this book in "the equipping of the saints for the work of ministry" (Eph. 4:12) and in enhancing the reputation of our bountifully generous heavenly Father.

—*Maylan Schurch*

Chapter Outline:

Welcome to the deeply fulfilling world of expository preaching! I've dwelt in this world for more than 20 years, and I can't imagine living anywhere else. Come on in! Before we go any further, let's get acquainted.

Does This Describe You?

- *You're an elder or other church volunteer.* But you've got a day job, too. Maybe you're a truck driver, a factory worker, a housecleaner, an engineer, a software programmer. Perhaps you're a mom with three kids. Or maybe you're even a sales and marketing executive who travels across the globe. Your pastor's very busy—and maybe he or she has more churches than just yours to care for, churches that need quality Bible-based sermons in the pastor's absence. (And perhaps the reason you're holding this book is that your pastor has just slapped it into your palm!)

- **You're a friend of a lay preacher** who's really working hard to prepare solid Bible messages—and his or her birthday's coming up! (Or Christmas, or Groundhog Day, or that next sermon assignment.)
- **You're a pastor.** As a result you either have several churches under your care, or a large church with too many satellite preaching opportunities to fulfill all by yourself. You know a few members who could preach really well if they had some instruction. Furthermore, your elders or church staff who are already preaching might be intrigued with a practical, entertaining guide to a sermon form they haven't yet tried.
- **You're a volunteer youth leader.** While you're not interested in doing a full-length sermon, just a 10-minute talk or devotional once in a while—you do want to put more Bible meat into it.
- **You're a prison ministry volunteer.** From firsthand experience you know how desperately your friends behind bars need encouraging, Bible-based messages during weekly worship services in the prison chapel. You're feeling called to fill that void.
- **You're a theology or seminary professor** who'd like to place in each homiletics student's hands a basic how-to book written by a pastor in the trenches who's been generating anywhere from 35 to 40 brandnew expository sermons every year for more than two decades.
- **You're a ministerial student** who'd like to grab this resource before it goes out of print!
- **You're a missionary.** Not only do you want to provide the virgin ears of your hearers with practical Bible truth; you also want to model how the Bible's treasures should be mined correctly.
- **You're a denominational leader,** and as part of your duties you're asked to circulate among several congregations and preach the worship service sermon. You may use the same message several times, so you'd like to make sure each one adequately feeds the flocks.
- **You're retired,** and your retirement center offers worship services—but not many pastors can spare the time to preach for them. Feeling the Lord guiding you to this ministry, you reverently want to develop this sacred calling.
- **You've never preached a sermon in your life,** and you'd like to learn how. Just for curiosity. Just in case. Or maybe you're just interested in

seeing "under the skin" of how a sermon is constructed so that you can get more out of the ones you hear.

- *Or maybe you're reading this book for some other reason* that I'd never be able to imagine!

Whoever you are, I think I can guarantee you a satisfying experience. Thanks for joining me!

Let Me Introduce Myself

The first thing I'd like to say is that a lot of other pastors could have written this book. Many godly preachers, both men and women, are carefully and prayerfully preparing weekly expository messages that satisfy the souls of their congregations. I'm certainly not the final expert—but during my 23 years of pastoring I've created and preached more than 600 brand-new, from-scratch expository sermons.

Just to make sure you know where I'm coming from, I don't pastor a megachurch. I'm the only paid pastor on my staff (but enjoy wonderful support from my wife, Shelley, and the scores of dedicated lay volunteers who serve in various ministries in my congregation). Somewhere between 160 and 180 people sit in my church sanctuary and listen to me every week. I've been in the same church for 15-plus years. I don't have a radio or TV ministry, and I'm not Max Lucado II. It's just that besides my pastoral experience I've had some background in book-writing, so I decided to seize this chance to pass on some of the things I've learned.

You see, I was a layperson until I was 32. I grew up in a tiny South Dakota congregation whose pastor had two other churches in his district. If our little group of worshippers was lucky, we got to hear him once every three weeks, but the rest of the time our local elders had to preach.

But one day—I think I was 19 years old—one of those elders kindly tapped me on the shoulder and asked me to get a sermon ready.

After my head had stopped whirling, and after he'd asked me again, I took the dare. And one frightening day I stood before the two dozen people in our congregation and desperately rattled off a long and boring message at woodpecker speed. Luckily I was too scared to study the expressions on my listeners' faces, because I'm sure they were hyperventilating right along with me. And trying not to smile.

But after the service was over—and once they'd caught their breath and lost that dizzy feeling—those precious people praised me to the skies. Wonder of wonders, the elder asked me to preach again. I gulped, agreed, and a few weeks later presented a slower and slightly more confident sermon.

And they kept asking for more, and I kept saying yes, and for the next several years I had the genuine pleasure of doing quite a bit of lay preaching. And even if God hadn't matched me up with a supportive, encouraging wife and then called me into the ministry, I still would have said yes whenever someone asked me to deliver a sermon.

As a full-time pastor for nearly the past quarter century, I've had the joy of challenging my own lay members to preach. I've seen their startled stares when I suggested it, and listened to their stunned protests. But then I noticed their confidence begin to grow as I gave them a bit of coaching. Finally, I've observed them bask in the same warmhearted congregational encouragement I received as a beginner.

I'm hoping you'll be willing to step into their ranks—because you're holding in your hands the book I wish I'd had when that elder first tapped me on the shoulder.

And Now a Word From My Brother About Armor

Before I go any further, I need to introduce you to my brother Chester, who has an important message for you.

Before I sent the final version of this manuscript to the publishers, I handed it out to several people for their suggestions. One of these was Pastor Chester Schurch, who serves a large church about 100 miles south of mine. I was very interested to see what he would say about it.

You see, Chester is seven years younger than I am. Even though he and I have the same last name—which is pronounced, believe it or not, "shirk"—and even though we were raised by the same parents in the same South Dakota farmhouse, it's as if we grew up in two different worlds. When I was a thoughtful college student up in my room reading a book, teenage Chester would be out behind our barn practicing basketball shots. While I barely remembered to keep gas and oil in my 1960 Chevy, Chester would later buff and polish and pinstripe his own first car.

Chester is more competitive, and I'm more laid-back. I taught him to play chess when he was 15, and in three months he was beating me almost every game. He tried to teach me basketball, but I just didn't have what it takes.

Because I came to the ministry from another career, he and I have been pastors for almost exactly the same amount of time—20-plus years. But he has pastored a wider variety of churches than I have, and therefore has gained more experience. Through the years he's developed his own very successful ways of working—some of them quite different from mine.

And that's true for how we prepare our sermons. At 5:00 each morning before I preach, I'm at my desk, reading my sermon manuscript aloud and making changes with a pen. But my brother has arisen even earlier, and is striding through the countryside preaching his sermon out loud, revising it phrase by phrase in his mind. Even though we both base our messages solidly on the Bible, Chester doesn't stay mainly with the expository style I'll be teaching you in this book. Instead, he uses a variety of patterns.

So after Chester read through this layperson's guide, we talked it over. He had several complimentary things to say. But he also said, "I guess what I would like your readers to remember is that we each have to preach in our own 'armor.'" He referred, of course, to the story of David and Goliath. Before David went out to fight the giant, King Saul donated his own suit of armor for the young man to use. David tried it on, but felt so uncomfortable that he finally left it behind and fought in his usual shepherd's garb.

And I'll echo what my brother says. Read this book. In it I will try earnestly to convince you that while my way isn't the only way, it's a good way. Absorb what you can use.

But then, under the guidance and blessing of God, go out and preach in your own armor.

An Important Cultural Caution

Sometimes preaching in your own armor means doing it in your own cultural armor. I'm a Caucasian male raised in America's Great Plains states among people of mostly German pioneer stock.

And I know that some of the solemn rules I lay down in these pages might cause African-Americans and Latinos and other non-Midwestern prairie boys to smile tolerantly—or even explode into laughter. "Sorry, Maylan," they'll say. "We're going to have to break some of your rules—because they're not what the people of our cultures will expect."

Amen. Pastors understand that *even within one culture* different congregations expect different preaching styles. But what I'm going to do in the pages ahead is to give the principles behind what I'm setting forth, so that you can intelligently adapt them to suit the needs of your people. Remember, *in any culture, you need to preach the Holy Bible as it reads. And in any culture you must earn the right to be heard.* I'm hoping that this book's principles will help you preach the Word, and earn the right to have people listen to it, no matter who you are or to whom you're speaking. And now, finally, it's time to start answering the question—

What Is Expository Preaching, and Why Is It So Important?

One of the reasons I'm having such fun writing this book is that I'm practicing what I preach. Right now. Literally. All week long I've been preparing an expository sermon on John 19. I've called it "Power Play," and tomorrow morning I'll be preaching it.

But I'm so excited about this layperson's guide that while I'm working on the "Power Play" sermon on one screen, I'm also hitting Alt-Tab every once in a while to shift over to this screen and add some more to the book.

But why *expository* sermons? Aren't there other sermon patterns?

There are. Before I define expository preaching for you, I'll mention four other popular formats:

- *The topical sermon.* This is the most common kind of sermon, and was the kind I prepared when as a layperson I was first asked to preach. In a topical sermon you first of all decide on a subject you want to cover, such as "The Love of God" or "How to Find Peace in Crisis." Then you hunt through the Bible for texts that talk about it and arrange them into an outline. Most traditional evangelistic sermons are topical.

- *The textual sermon.* This is the sermon in which you choose one Bible verse, such as John 3:16, and preach through it phrase by phrase. First you discuss how "God so loved the world," next you explore the gift of "His only begotten Son," and then you examine the meaning of "whosoever believes," and so on. *Warning:* a textual sermon gets a bit thin unless you carefully bring in other Bible passages to support what you're saying.

- *The narrative sermon.* "A narrative sermon," says *The Concise Encyclopedia of Preaching,* "is any sermon in which the arrangement of ideas takes the form of a plot involving a strategic delay of the preacher's meaning."[1] *Narrative* is a sort of umbrella term. I think that through the years I've developed something of a narrative style, though I most often give it an expository topspin. The best thing you can do right now is to get basic training in how to unpack and present principles from good-sized Bible passages—which this layperson's guide will definitely help you do.

- *The dramatic monologue.* In this sermon you pretend to be a Bible character: "As I crouched by the fire in the courtyard, I heard a young woman's voice behind me. 'Weren't you with Jesus of Nazareth? Aren't you one of His disciples?'" Two warnings: This approach takes a lot of work and rehearsal to make it effective. Also, you won't want to use it every week. Once or twice a year is plenty.

Warning! Don't preach the "Sermon That Pretends to Be Expository."
Before I go any further, I'm going to introduce you to a *bad* example of a sermon style. The reason I bring this up is that some people who use this format think they're preaching expository sermons. This bad sermon style is—

- *The running-commentary sermon (RCS).* The speaker reads a verse, talks a little about it, then reads the next verse, and discusses it a bit, and so on, *but with no main idea, and no focused plan or outline.* The reason the RCS sometimes gets mistaken for an expository sermon is that it can cover a lot of ground—several texts, or even a whole chapter. But as I say, it often has no central theme—no clear destination. And once the hostages (I mean, the *listeners*) sense this rudderless approach, they get a despairing feeling in their chests and start looking at their watches. And finally, 10 minutes beyond the usual sermon-stopping time, the running commentator looks at the clock. "Where has all the time gone?" he gasps. Everybody else in the room *knows.* They've lived through each weary, aimless minute.

So what's an expository sermon?
First, I'm going to step back and let a couple of experts define it, and then I'll break it down. (Alert: the next paragraph is fairly heavy going. *But do not put down the book.* Just fasten your seat belts, and I'll clear things up once we're through it.)

The Expository Sermon Defined

The Concise Encyclopedia of Preaching gives a good general definition: "The expository sermon is a sermon which faithfully brings a message out of scripture and makes that message accessible to contemporary hearers."[2] Expository preaching guru Haddon Robinson goes a bit further—and here's where you need the seat belt: "Expository preaching is the communication of a biblical concept, derived from and transmitted through a historical, grammatical, and literary study of a passage in its context which the Holy Spirit first applies to the personality and experience of the preacher, then through [the preacher] to [the] hearers."[3]

OK, relax now. Unclick that seat belt. Believe it or not, in spite of the impressive, well-buffed language above, *you too can preach an expository sermon*. Starting in the next chapter I'll show you how, step by step. I just wanted you to get a feel—from a couple of preaching's "big guns"—for how really important and satisfying it is.

Let's boil it down:

In a nutshell, an expository sermon starts with a good-sized passage of Scripture, such as a chapter, and draws its topic and its points totally from that passage.

Do you see the difference between this and a topical or textual sermon or dramatic monologue or running commentary? A dramatic monologue isn't so much a sermon as a mini stage play. A topical sermon starts when you bring your own subject to the Bible and start gathering texts to support it. A textual sermon has the danger of trying to draw too much from too little. A running commentary is a rambling, unfocused time-waster—it's the type of "sermon" after which if you ask someone who's heard it what it was about, he or she will say, "Uh . . . let's see . . . I'm not really sure." In other words, very forgettable.

But an expository sermon starts with a Bible chapter or other longish passage, and finds and develops a focused topic from within it. In fact, once you learn how to preach in this style, you will immediately be able to share with your listeners the five benefits of expository preaching.

Five Priceless Benefits of Expository Preaching

- *If you preach expository, you'll be presenting the Bible the way its inspired authors composed it.* When John sat down to write his Gospel, he had a specific flow of thought in mind. He had ideas he intended to develop step by step. If he had wanted us only to know John 3:16, he could have just printed up T-shirts or bumper stickers rather than embedding that verse in an entire book! John wished us to understand that it was to the Pharisee Nicodemus that Jesus first spoke John 3:16. The disciple meant for us to read Nicodemus' questions and to hear Jesus' answers, with verse 16 coming as something of a climax. So when you preach an expository message, you're allowing your hearers the most direct and dependable access to the Bible.

- *If you preach expository, you'll be modeling how to read and interpret the Bible.* Too many people these days find themselves intimidated by Bible study. They assume that only the experts can interpret Scripture correctly,

18

and this leaves them open to deception by anyone with a loud voice and an ego and a one-track mind. When I was a layperson, I remember being startled and refreshed every time I heard an expository message. I listened to it far more carefully than I did other kinds of sermons, because I sensed that it had less chance of its speakers being able to bend the Bible to their will. It was this kind of sermon that always encouraged me to read Scripture as a connected narrative rather than "a text here and a text there."

- **If you preach expository, nobody can accuse you of "proof-texting."** Proof-texting is coming up with an idea, locating one Bible verse or part of a verse, and using it to try to back that idea up. For example, someone might tell you that the Bible approves of polygamy, and they'll quote you verses about Abraham and Jacob and their multiple wives. But a wider view of the Bible shows that polygamy wasn't God's original plan.

Two weeks ago I discovered to my surprise that for years I had been proof-texting Isaiah 55:8, 9: " 'For My thoughts are not your thoughts, nor are your ways My ways,' says the Lord. 'For as the heavens are higher than the earth, so are My ways higher than your ways, and My thoughts than your thoughts.' "

Every time I quoted that verse in my sermons I would say something like this: "Since God's ways and thoughts are so much higher than ours, we'd probably better just trust Him with the things we can't yet understand." And of course that's true—anyone who could create both an awesome universe and a fantastically functioning human body *does* have vastly greater intelligence than the people He created. However, in these verses God was *not* trying to prove His superior intelligence. Just read them in their context, and you'll see that He was stating just how superhumanly *forgiving and pardoning* He is.

- **When you preach expository, you'll help protect your hearers from dangerous heresies.** And that's because you're allowing them to see that in their contexts Bible passages do make sense, and that careful readers can follow Scripture's ways of reasoning. The more a congregation gets to watch this happen, the more subconsciously alert they'll be to any funny business on the part of someone who later tries to get them to believe something that doesn't have solid Bible backing.
- **When you preach expository, you may be giving your hearers the only "Bible" they'll be getting all week.** Scary but true. So give them Bible—and interpret it well.

Ready for a change of pace? Let me respond to some questions that might have popped up as you read this chapter.

Questions You Might Be Having

Maybe you still have the same dizzy feeling I had when someone first asked me to preach. And maybe some questions are nibbling at your mind. Let me guess:

- *"Shouldn't we leave preaching to career pastors?"* No. Almost all of the preachers in the Bible were *laypersons,* not salaried pastors. None of Jesus' disciples had theology degrees. Even Pharisee Paul was a layperson whose day job was making tents. And what's interesting is that in order to be an effective gospel presenter, he actually had to *unlearn* a good bit of his rabbinical training! God called Bible lay preachers because He needed His Word revealed in a clear, credible, down-to-earth way.

One of my friends who read the first draft of this book said to me, "When I was younger, I always thought that 'preaching' should be done by pastors. I thought that if a layperson spoke from the pulpit, it should be a 'talk,' not a 'sermon.'" If that's bothering you, glance back at the previous paragraph. In the Bible, laypersons *preached.* Fisherman Peter didn't give a "talk" at Pentecost. Tentmaker Paul didn't present "talks" as he defended his newfound Friend, Jesus. These laypersons *preached sermons.*

- *"A lot of people in my congregation have more education than I do."* Not to worry. The Holy Spirit, speaking through the Bible, is where the wisdom and the power come from. An experienced pastor who read this manuscript commented, "Here's something I like to tell lay preachers afraid that others in the congregation might know more than they do: none of your listeners has studied this topic deeply in order to present it. There may be smarter people listening who know more, but they still haven't spent the time on the subject that you have. I pick up information from my members all the time. They put a twist on a topic that I never considered. Don't feel intimidated, just humbled in speaking for God."

Another thing to remember is this: as long as you deliver your message humbly, and preach the truth as though it were being spoken to you as well as to the congregation, their attention will be focused where it should be: on Jesus and not on you. Remember how, when Jesus healed the sick, people glorified not Him but God (Matt. 9:8). Pray that the same thing happens when you preach.

- *"Don't I need to know Greek and Hebrew in order to interpret God's Word correctly?"* No. If God thought everybody had to read the New Testament in its original tongue, He would have made Greek the world language. Instead, what you need are three to five literal translations of the Bible. (What I mean by "literal" is how close the translation is to a word-for-word reproduction of the original Greek or Hebrew.) In English they would include the King James Version, the New King James Version, the *New American Standard Bible,* the Revised Standard Version, and the English Standard Version. If your own language doesn't have many literal translations, find the most literal one or two you can, and study from them. By prayerfully studying your Bible passage in each of these translations, you'll have what you need. (I'll talk about helpful Bible reference tools later in the book.)

- *"How can I preach if I get stage fright when I speak in front?"* I got stage fright as a young lay preacher, even standing in front of the warm, supportive congregation I'd grown up in. Then I minored in speech in college, and discovered the secret: if you're well prepared, and if you rehearse two or three times, 80 percent of your nervousness will vanish. And what's left is *good*—it's that little shot of adrenaline that keeps you on your toes! So don't write yourself off as a public speaker until you allow this book and the Holy Spirit to prepare you to preach at least two or three expository sermons.

- *"But who will listen to what I have to say?"* Your entire congregation. And they may respond to you with even greater interest than they do to your pastor! They'll be rooting for you—because you're from the pewside of the pulpit. You're one of *them.* And this book will help you become a far more interesting speaker than they ever dreamed you could be.

- *"How can I get an opportunity to preach?"* Very carefully. Of course, if your pastor has given you this book, it means that he or she has confidence in you, and might already have a pulpit date in mind. But if this whole preaching idea started with you, keep in mind that pastors are pretty choosy about who occupies their pulpits—and that's because *they're* the ones who'll get beaten about the head and shoulders (figuratively speaking) if a lay preacher turns out to be nothing more than an ego with a mouth or a crafty spreader of heresies.

I'd suggest that you go to your pastor and say, "I just got hold of this book, and I'm considering working through it and preparing a sermon.

Can you think of anywhere I might be able to preach it?" Chances are, if you haven't caused trouble that the pastor has had to mop up, you'll be given some ideas. A lot of this hangs on your reputation. (If you do get a preaching date, make sure it's six to eight weeks away if possible. If it's closer, it's still doable, but you'll be really scrambling!)

And by the way, if you're working on a sermon right now, I've created a section at the end of most chapters just for you, after the homework projects.

OK. Enough for now. In the next chapter I'll start sharing my own rubber-meets-the-road method for creating an expository sermon that people will listen to. And I'll show you how to start assembling a couple sermon preparation kits. But now here's some fun and vitally important research to do. Please don't skip this.

Homework Project 1—Sermon Evaluation

In the appendix at the end of this book you'll find a Sermon Evaluation Form. Enlarge it on a photocopier to 8½" x 11" size so it'll be easier to use. Bring it with you to your church next worship service (or visit another church) and use it to evaluate the pastor's sermon. The reason you're doing this is so that you can discover good practices to imitate as well as other practices you'd like to avoid. *Please remember to fold the bottom half of the form underneath, and don't fill it out until the next day.* (That way you can evaluate how easy the pastor's message was to remember.)

Get a Preaching Date

If your pastor handed you this book, he or she may already have a date in mind. Make sure it's about six to eight weeks away, because you'll need the time to do this right, though you could probably prepare your sermon in a month or even less if you had to. Should your pastor not be aware that you have this book, let him or her know. Ask for advice on how and where you could preach the sermon you create from this book.

If You're Working on a Sermon Right Now

Should you already be actually preparing a sermon, always check the "If You're Working on a Sermon Right Now" segment at the end of each chapter. It should help keep you on track so you'll have a completed sermon by the time you're through chapter 12.

But right now, here's what you should be concentrating on: daily prayer that the Lord will guide in your search for a Bible chapter to preach on. If you've already chosen one, pray that He'll help you create an effective sermon—or direct you to another chapter of Scripture that would be better.

GROUP DISCUSSION STARTERS

If you're going through this book along with other people, and you're meeting together to discuss it, here are some possible topics to consider. *Materials that may be needed for discussion times:* pencils and pens, and paper, plus a blackboard or whiteboard or flipchart and chalk or markers.

Get acquainted. (If you know each other already, skip this.) The goal is for everybody to know everybody else's name by the time this exercise is over. Give everyone a piece of paper and ask them to make a seating chart and to keep it in front of them during the session.

Glance again at the "Does This Describe You?" section. Group members should be ready to say in a few sentences why they've joined the group and what they hope to gain from it.

Close your layperson's guide. Take paper and pencil and, without peeking at the book, write a one-sentence definition of expository preaching. After everyone's done, read it aloud and compare answers.

Using pencil and paper—or one of the back pages of this book—list your three major worries about preaching a sermon. Leave space after each worry so that later, after you've preached, you can describe whether the worry was valid, or whether things turned out better than you thought they might. Discuss your concerns with the group.

Look at Homework Project 1. Try to make sure that evaluations will be made on as many different speakers as possible, even if it means attending a church of another denomination this weekend. The goal is to analyze the preaching habits of many different people. (Next time the group should discuss them as anonymously as possible.)

---

[1] *The Concise Encyclopedia of Preaching,* ed. William H. Willimon and Richard Lischer (Louisville: Westminster John Knox Press, 1995).

[2] *Ibid.,* pp. 130, 131.

[3] Haddon Robinson, *Biblical Preaching: The Development and Delivery of Expository Messages,* 2nd ed. (Grand Rapids: Baker Academic, 2001).

2

Chapter Outline:

A Former Layperson Listens to a Sermon

I mentioned in the previous chapter that I was a layperson until I was 32. That means I've listened to a whole lot of sermons from the pewside of the pulpit.

Want to hear a shocker? *I can't remember a single sermon I ever heard.*

Wait. Don't drop this book in discouragement. That's natural. Can you remember what your pastor preached about two weeks ago? Pastors, can you remember what you presented two weeks ago? (If somebody asked *me* that question, I'd have to go find that particular day's church bulletin and look at the sermon title!)

Don't get me wrong. I'm not glorifying forgetfulness. You and I need to immerse our minds in our Bibles more than we're probably doing right now. As we listen to sermons—or prepare them—we need to say to ourselves, "This week I'm going to try to put these Bible truths to work. I'm going to make a conscious effort to think about them and apply them."

However, I don't think you have to be able to repeat the details of a sermon in order for it to have an effect on you. I believe that if you *listen* to a sermon, its information gets stored somewhere in the electronic archives of your mind. And later, little bits and pieces of it rise back to the surface, maybe in a Bible class discussion or in a conversation with someone at work. You most likely won't remember where those tidbits came from, but they're there, ready for use.

If.

Notice the big *If?* Those pieces of information and insight will come back to you only *if* the sermon was interesting and tightly connected enough to keep you focused on it in the first place.

And that's why I'm going to take a moment and list some of my own sermonic pet peeves and pleasures. Trust me—even though I'm a pastor, I can get just as bored, just as frustrated, and just as wristwatch-fixated as you can when someone's sermon isn't working for me.

How to Keep Maylan Happily Awake When You Preach

- *Tell me stories.* You've seen it happen a hundred times. A speaker is droning along, and suddenly he says, "A couple of summers ago my wife and I took a trip to Yellowstone—" Immediately heads jerk up all over the sanctuary, and we gaze alertly at him, waiting to hear what happened.

  I'm not saying your sermon should be one long string of stories. Well-thought-out sentences and good transitions will rivet the attention too. Just don't forget to include stories. Later I'll show you how to do it effectively.

  And while we're on the subject of stories—

- *Don't tell me stories that never happened and pretend that they're true.* I once heard a preacher tell about how a woman was trying to get her kitten down from a small tree. She reached up and pulled some branches down toward her, hoping she could grab the cat with her other hand. The branches slipped from her hand, catapulting the kitten into the air. It landed a few seconds later in the backyard of a couple who had been praying for a kitten. Moral: the Lord sometimes answers prayers in dramatic and funny ways.

  Problem. As I remember it, this pastor told the story as though it had happened to a friend of his.

  Problem. I had heard that same story told by a Christian actress on a videotaped seminar she'd presented several years earlier as having occurred to her relatives. And I've heard that story three or four times since, by people who claimed it to be an experience of friends of *theirs*.

Problem. The story is inherently implausible. A kitten hurled any great distance would have died from the shock of hitting the ground.

It's OK to tell a parable—but if you do, signal strongly to us that this is what it is. And by all means, don't pretend your story happened to you yourself when it didn't. Get the reputation of telling the truth in your sermons, even though it might not be as exciting.

- *Surprise me.* Don't preach me a predictable sermon about Christian duty in which your three points are "Study your Bible," "Pray," and "Share." While those are all good things, and we're Laodicean Christians without them, dig deep into the verses *behind* those concepts and tell me things that I never suspected. Include details I've never thought of before. Help explode the erroneous idea that the Bible is a boring book full of shabby clichés.
- *Use humor.* Laughter in the sanctuary *is not wrong*. Of course, don't feed me 10 minutes of comic one-liners. Don't start nosing around in a joke book for material. Instead, do your best to find warmhearted humor in the Bible passage. For example, when you're preaching about Israel's deliverance from Egypt, let your mind dwell for a moment on those frogs hopping around on Pharaoh's palace floor. His kids probably loved it, but his wife was going crazy. And imagine Pharaoh himself trying to hold high-level political talks and having to read his agenda from a scroll dotted with soggy frogprints.

When people chuckle, pause. Let them enjoy the laugh. And as the mirth begins to die, start talking again. Get serious. Resist the temptation to "milk" the laugh with follow-up one-liners as a comedian would.

- *Show me that you like me.* Smile naturally at me. Look at me. Talk as if you're on my side of the pulpit with me, and that the Bible is speaking to both of us. Don't thunder from Sinai. Instead, signal to me that you too are wading hip-deep through the real world, and that even though you still have questions, God has helped you wrestle with reality.
- *Assure me that God loves me.* You'll never know how bruised and bleeding my heart may be. I need to know—from the Bible—that God really adores me, yes, even *me*. Because life's tough, and Satan is savagely cruel.
- *Don't preach your sermon as if you're reading it.* If you write it out word for word, as I do mine, practice it enough so that you can glance down at

the page, scoop up an entire sentence, and deliver it completely—and naturally—into the ears of your congregation. Then glance down and grab another one.

Well, if I keep this up I won't have anything to talk about in the rest of the book! But those are the "biggies," to my way of thinking.

Now—one more very important matter to consider before we get better acquainted with expository preaching.

Preparing the Preacher

Don't skip this part.

I say this because every good how-to-preach book I've ever read includes a chapter on the preacher's spiritual life. And the authors always put that chapter first, before going on to the preaching instruction. And after 23 years in the ministry, I've come to the conclusion that if you're trying to preach without going through the steps I'm about to mention, the Lord isn't going to be able to use you nearly as effectively, because you'll be a hypocrite—and you know what Jesus thought of hypocrites. So here are the steps. I'll keep them short and sweet.

- *Recommit your life to Jesus.* Tell the Lord you know that you're a sinner. Confess your sins. Ask for His forgiveness and for His Holy Spirit power to help you live a godly life.

- *Stop harboring known sin.* Are you reading magazines, watching videos, visiting Web sites you shouldn't? Are you financially dishonest? Are you eating or drinking (or injecting or smoking) things you shouldn't? Do you have an unforgiving nature? Are you breaking one or more of the Ten Commandments in thought, word, or deed? Do you feel apathy toward people that Jesus died for? Are you a saint at church and a monster at home? Are you in the habit of doing or saying or thinking anything else you know could short-circuit the Holy Spirit's ability to work through you?

If any of that is even vaguely true, go back to step 1 and turn all this over to the Lord. Confess your weaknesses and claim promises such as Hebrews 8:10. We've got to live by a higher standard if we're standing in the pulpit proclaiming God's Word. Because a lot of young people will be watching us (including our own kids, if we have them), and their young stomachs will twist into bitter knots if we're hypocrites.

But don't stop preparing your sermon! You don't have to be *perfect* to preach (remember Paul's continuing agony over his own soul), but every day you should humbly commit your life and your actions to the Lord, and live as if He means the world to you.

- *Get a daily devotional time going again.* Here's what I do. It's worked for me for quite a while, and it's simple. I set my alarm a half hour earlier than normal. Then, when it awakens me, I take a Bible, a prayer notebook, and a digital kitchen timer downstairs to the living room couch. I set the timer and start it going.

First I glance over past prayers I've recorded, and if I have received answers I jot them down. Then I think of new things or people to pray for, and write those down, and pray for them. Then for the rest of the time until the timer beeps, I just read my Bible. I have a little chart taped inside its back cover, where I mark off chapters I've finished. I jump around a lot—a book in the New Testament, then one in the Old. It's tempting to "cheat" and use this time to read the passage I'm going to be preaching on, but I don't do that. This time is just between me and God.

Here's what this does for me. Not only does it allow me to read the Bible in a relaxed and restful way, and not only does it give me thunderously amazing insights once in a while, but it also keeps me honest. And later, when I'm working on my sermon, I have a feeling of integrity, because I've connected with the Lord through the pages of His Word. I don't feel like a hollow-hearted hypocrite.

- *Pray about your sermons.* Right now, before you write even the first of your expository sermons, pray that the Lord will use them to mature you, and then to reach the people with His will. Pray this every time you work on a new one.

Now, in the preceding chapter I promised you that I would start telling you how to create an expository sermon.

How Would You Like to Worship With . . .

- *A congregation that has a growing confidence* that the Bible can provide real answers for their lives?
- *A congregation that's increasingly fortified* against deceptive heresies?
- *A pastor whose workload and stress are eased* because informed laypersons are helping preach?

Did you answer yes? Of course you did. And I'll bet you can guess one of the things that under God's blessing will help produce these happy outcomes: expository preaching. And in your case, *lay* expository preaching.

Notice, I didn't say lay *preaching*. I said lay *expository* preaching. Because—and I've sung this song before and I'll sing as many verses as I have to—I believe that every Christian congregation needs a steady diet of expository sermons. Sure, you can preach a topical or textual or dramatic monologue sermon once in a while, but expository sermons are the staff of life to any group of believers.

"So show me how an expository sermon is organized," you say.

I'm so glad you asked! Here's the bare-bones outline for the basic expository sermon. *Don't be intimidated. I'll talk you through it.*

The Classic Expository Sermon

It should include the following segments:

Introduction
Transition
SPICAT
SPICAT
SPICAT

One more SPICAT if absolutely necessary

Conclusion/Appeal

What's a SPICAT?

"What on earth," you ask, "is a SPICAT?"

I thought I'd invented that acronym, until I found out it's also a Latin word. *Spica* means both "a spike" and "an ear of corn." I'd like to think of every sermon SPICAT as a "spike," helping to fasten a Bible truth firmly to the walls of your hearers' minds, and as a nourishing "ear" of corn on the cob that helps them grow spiritually.

SPICAT stands for:

S cripture
P oint
I llustration
C omments
A pplication
T ransition

Think of It as a Recipe

"Uh-oh," you might be saying to yourself. "This sounds complicated."

Really, it's not. Just think of it as a recipe. The same day I was working on the "Power Play" sermon I mentioned in the previous chapter, I took a break to help my wife prepare potluck food. She was using a recipe that one of our members had given her, one that was even longer than the SPICAT list above. Shelley wasn't rattled, though—she just methodically worked her way through the directions, and the result was delightful.

In the same way, the above expository sermon recipe will soon become second nature to you. Once you've notched three or four sermons into your belt, you'll barely even have to look at the recipe.

So what's a SPICAT?

A SPICAT is *one fleshed-out sermon point.*

For example, a three-point sermon would have three SPICATs. And the nice thing is, you can use SPICAT with topical or textual sermons, too—it's simply a balanced and satisfying way of delivering a portion of Bible truth to people. (How do you pronounce SPICAT? Any way you want to. I call it SPY-cat, but you can pronounce it SPEE-cat or SPIH-cat if you want.)

In the chapters ahead I will walk you through the whole recipe in detail, but let me flesh it out a bit more right here so that you can see where we're going.

Remember, with expository preaching you're starting not with a text or a topic, but a good-sized portion of Scripture, such as a chapter.

- **The Introduction** is an attention-getting story or quote or question that focuses your hearers on the main idea you've discovered in your Scripture passage.
- **The Transition** ties of the introduction to the main idea. Part of your transition will contain the extremely crucial "approach sentence."
  (Now here's where the SPICAT starts.)
- **The Scripture** is the verse or verses that contain your first point. You read the scripture first, then you introduce—
- **The Point.** This is the first major statement you're making about your Bible passage. Once you've stated your point, launch into—
- **The Illustration.** This is a story or other interesting item that gives an example of your point. Jesus used many illustrations. Rather than merely saying "God will take care of you," He pointed to the lilies of the field. And rather than simply declaring, "God longs for the wandering sinner

30

to return," He told the story of the prodigal son. The sermon point reaches the mind—but the illustration touches the heart. *Do not neglect to include illustrations.* (Later I'll tell you how to find good ones.)

- **The Comments.** Here's where you expand on the point. For example, if you're preaching on a Bible story, you now tell what at first puzzled you or startled you or encouraged you about the Scripture segment you've just read. It is a good place to include some information about life in Bible times, to enhance your hearers' understanding.
- **The Application.** Now you begin to answer such questions as How does this apply to me, right here, right now? How can I make this practical? What are some action steps I can take to put this to work Monday morning? *The application is often the hardest part of preparing a sermon, but trust me: if you neglect it, your hearers will leave the service unsatisfied.* As a pastor friend of mine observes: "If it's of no use on Monday, why say it in the sermon?" I'll talk more about applications in a later chapter.
- **The Transition.** Finished with one SPICAT, you smoothly tie it to your next SPICAT. Don't neglect the transition, because if you do, the sermon stops "flowing" and gets jerky, and people will start to yawn and peek at their watches. In recent years I've worked hard to improve my own transitions, and it's really made a difference. A good transition compels your hearers to keep focused—they just can't help listening.

Once you're done with your transition, you launch right into the next SPICAT, and then the next one. Don't put any more than three or four SPICATs in a sermon. And by the way, your listeners will bless you if you finish the entire sermon *within 30 minutes.*

The 30-Minute Rule

"Hey, that's not me!" I can hear somebody yelping in alarm. "I can't get my point across in under *40* minutes."

"This is cultural," said one of my manuscript evaluators, who's African-American. "In the Black cultures a 30-minute message is a 'sermonette.' As a famous Black preacher once said: 'Sermonettes make Christianettes.' Most times 'typical' sermons last 45 minutes to an hour. Congregations from this cultural background expect more."

OK, I'll allow some wiggle room here. Consider the following guideline, however:

Don't preach longer than your pastor normally does, if he or she goes beyond

31

30 minutes. In fact, maybe a good rule of thumb is to knock 25 percent of your pastor's sermon length off your own message. One reason this might be a good idea is that he or she is probably very experienced at holding people's attention, and you're just learning. Another reason for making your own sermon shorter is that *you need to earn the right to be heard.* The African-American evaluator I mentioned above says that for beginners in his own culture, 30 minutes might indeed be a good target length.

Now, cultural differences aside, I'm going to use 30 minutes as the ideal in this book—because that's the "armor" I myself preach in. In fact, in many Caucasian congregations sermons are even shorter these days. So even if you come from an extended-sermon culture, please stay tuned, because conciseness and focus will always be useful no matter how long your sermons eventually become.

In a nutshell, staying within a time frame is most often a matter of eliminating that extra SPICAT or two you don't really need. (Important rule of thumb: *It is generally better to eliminate a SPICAT than it is to try to downsize the others to make the sermon fit within a half hour.*)

Why 30 minutes or less? Life may be thrilling for us preachers up behind the pulpit. We're the center of attention, and we get to do all the talking. But time is passing, and no matter how politely your friends gaze at you, they're getting restless. Moms with squirmy kids are deep in prayer: *Lord, help this speaker wrap it up.*

I mentioned eliminating SPICATs to save time. In one out of every three sermons I prepare, I have to skip over SPICATs. I eliminated one yesterday, as a matter of fact, while working on a John 20 sermon called "The *First* Second Coming." The SPICAT I dumped was a fairly weak one, and its departure tightened the outline nicely.

Another important rule of thumb: *Don't be obsessive about getting through the entire Bible chapter you're preaching on.* Just give your hearers three or four good SPICATs, and keep it all under 30 minutes.

Once you've preached through your SPICATs, it's time for—

- **The Conclusion/Appeal.** You'll be strongly tempted to leave this out. Maybe you've worked so hard on the sermon that you don't have a lot of energy left to create the conclusion. Or perhaps you're a little shy about making an appeal. I'll talk more about appeals later. They don't all have to be come-forward calls, if that's what's worrying you. Just make sure you include some opportunity for your audience to respond.

Now you've got the basic framework. I'll go into a lot more detail later. In the next chapter I'll give some guidelines for choosing a biblical chapter to preach on. I'll also suggest two "sermon preparation kits," and offer you hints about collecting and using illustrations.

Homework Project 2—Choosing Your Preaching Chapters

Start thinking about two or three separate chapters, from different parts of the Bible, that you might be interested in using to prepare an expository message. (Choose just *one* of these chapters for your sermon, of course.) The reason I suggest two or three is so you won't have put all your eggs in a single basket if one of your chapters doesn't work out. In just a few pages I'll give you some guidelines to help you settle on a Scripture passage if you don't have any in mind.

If You're Working on a Sermon Right Now

- *Keep praying* that the Lord will help you create an effective sermon.
- *Pray your way through* the "Preparing the Preacher" steps in this chapter.

GROUP DISCUSSION STARTERS

Bring with you the sermon evaluation forms you filled out on the speaker you listened to, and carefully and charitably comment on them. *Very important:* during this discussion, have someone assigned to compile a list of sermon do's and don'ts based on the evaluations.

Think back to past sermons you've listened to (besides the one you evaluated). Do you remember anything about those sermons, any parts of them? If so, tell what you remember, and with the group's help come up with some suggestions about why those particular details stuck in your memory.

On one of the blank pages of your preaching book—or on a separate piece of paper—write a prayer. Begin it "Dear Jesus," or "Dear heavenly Father," and recommit your life and any future sermon you might preach to Them. Allow 15 minutes for this. Group members may read them aloud if they feel comfortable doing so.

Share ways of doing a daily devotional time, even if you're not doing it that way now. What works for you? What doesn't?

Take another look at the sermon evaluation forms. Each evaluator should be prepared to say whether the sermon preached by his or her pastor was too long, too short, or about right—and to give reasons.

3

Chapter Outline:

The Flashlight Story

Once upon a time, when I was a solemn-faced seminary student, I learned a valuable lesson. I was walking across campus and happened to fall into conversation with a woman who'd lived in the area for a long time.

"So you're training to be a preacher, are you?" she asked.

"That's right."

She glanced thoughtfully at me. Then she pointed at the huge campus church at the far end of the lawn.

"I've been attending that church for more than 20 years," she said. "I've heard sermons from all the major speakers and preachers and evangelists in our denomination. But there's only one sermon I remember."

My ears perked up.

"And it wasn't a sermon by one of the 'stars,'" she continued. "One of our associate pastors was speaking that day." She mentioned his name, but I'd never heard it before.

She went on to tell me that the pastor had brought a flashlight into the pulpit.

"I know this flashlight is a good one," he had said to the thousand or so people gathered there. "I know the light bulb is good. The batteries are new, and the switch on the handle is working."

He thumbed the switch several times, but the bulb stayed dark. "H'mmm," he said. "I wonder what's wrong." Shaking the flashlight, he turned it sideways and upside down. No light. Finally he unscrewed the cap at the end of the battery compartment. "Aha. Here's the problem. It's a little piece of paper caught between the bottom battery and the contact on the cap." Removing the paper, he screwed the flashlight back together, and it worked perfectly.

The woman concluded her story. "The pastor went on to tell us that the little piece of paper was like known sin in our lives. It may seem so small that we scarcely recognize that it's there. But it can hamper the Holy Spirit from letting us be lights in the world."

And among all the sermons by the powerful pulpit-pounders and brilliant logicians and passionate evangelists she'd listened to, that was the only one she remembered.

Which is why illustrations are so important. I'll be discussing them later in the chapter. But first we need something to illustrate, so let's talk about—

How to Choose a Preaching Passage

"All Scripture," declares 2 Timothy 3:16, "is given by inspiration of God, and is profitable for doctrine, for reproof, for correction, for instruction."

All Scripture. All 1,189 chapters. That means that neither you nor I will ever run out of preaching material. But if you're a beginning preacher, how do you decide which chapter to start with?

Here are some suggestions.

- *Pray that the Lord will guide you to the right passage.* He'll expect you, of course, to use your God-given mind and power of choice and creative instinct, so don't wait for Him to feed you your sermon word for word from on high. But start the process with a prayer, such as: "Lord, I'm not doing this to inflate my ego. I'm doing it so that people will glorify You. Please guide me to the chapter that will best do this right now." And then consider the following suggestions:

- *Preach on the Bible chapter that contains your favorite Bible story.* Get ready to be greatly surprised at the additional insights you'll find there, especially if you haven't read that story for several years. Or better yet, go to the children's Bible classes and have *them* vote on what Bible story you should preach on! Guess who'll be your most interested hearers the day you speak!

- *Ask yourself the sobering question "If I knew that I was going to die within the hour, and I could choose just one Bible chapter to read, what would it be?"* Prepare your sermon on that chapter, and make sure we understand why it's so vital to you.

- *Preach on a Bible chapter that relates to a nearby holiday.* Is Easter approaching? Maybe your pastor will be doing the major sermon that weekend, but if you're speaking a few weeks early, your sermon could be "How I'm Getting Ready for Easter," or (if afterward) "What This Easter Meant to Me." July 4 is an ideal time for a "freedom in Christ" message. Any good calendar store or appointment book will keep you posted on both major and minor holidays. Maybe a Jewish holiday is coming up, such as Rosh Hashanah or Purim. They offer great opportunities to find Bible chapters on those events, and let you relate them to Christ and the gospel.

- *Preach on a Bible chapter that deals with a topic related to "this day in history."* Once you get a preaching date, ask your librarian to show you where the "this day in history" reference materials are, or search online with the words "this day in history." Let that day's events lead you to an appropriate Bible chapter. Your hearers will be intrigued to hear you say, "On this very day 350 years ago . . ."

- *Tell your conversion or recommitment story.* Again, to make this an expository sermon you'll need to find a Bible chapter to base it on. Preach on that chapter—but use your spiritual experience to illustrate it. And try to make your conversion at least as exciting as all the bad things you did before the Lord got through to you!

- *Ask your pastor if you can fit your message to his or her sermon series.* Maybe your pastor has been preaching through the book of Matthew and will take a week off. Suggest that you might fill the gap by preaching on what would be that week's chapter.

These are just a few ideas to get you going. The main thing—if you haven't done it already—is to get Homework Project 3 going right away:

Start thinking about two or three separate chapters, from different parts of the Bible, that you might be interested in preaching from. (You'll be focusing on just *one* of these chapters per sermon, of course.)

Warning! Two Things *Not* to Preach About!

- *Don't preach about a current denominational or local church crisis.* Such things should be handled in other settings and by other people. It might be tempting to get your personal opinion off your chest in a public way, but any worship service sermon should rise far above that. People come to church bruised and beaten up by a tough week, and they don't need to get kicked around anymore.

  When one of my lay preacher friends read the above paragraph, he wrote, "Beautiful!" and reminded me of Isaiah 40:1, 2:

> "Comfort, yes, comfort My people!"
> Says your God.
> "Speak comfort to Jerusalem, and cry out to her,
> That her warfare is ended,
> That her iniquity is pardoned."

You will help heal wounded hearts if you choose a preaching chapter far removed from the issues of the crisis. Preach about Jesus in such a way that your hearers will leave the room with some of His "peace that passes understanding."

- *Don't preach about politics.* Get out your magnifying glass and scour the Sermon on the Mount, and you'll never catch Jesus calling for the overthrow of Palestine's Roman occupiers. You'll never find Peter taking sides in the political struggles between Jerusalem's mayor and city council. And what did *Paul* preach about? All together now: "Jesus Christ and Him crucified" (1 Cor. 2:2).

  Now let's start assembling—

Your Sermon Preparation Kits

Kits, plural. Two, to be exact.

Why two kits? Because one you'll carry with you, and the other you'll leave at home. You'll be twice as successful with both—and only one fourth as successful if you try to use just one.

The Carry-along Kit

You'll use this kit to help you work on your sermon "on the fly." Take with you some photocopies of your sermon chapter, a little stack of note cards (or a notebook of some kind), and a pen or pencil. The reason for this is that once you've focused on a Bible chapter, and once you've convinced yourself to preach on it, your God-created subconscious mind will start telegraphing all sorts of ideas or insights (workable and unworkable) to you, and you'll need some way to catch and record them before they vanish—*which they will,* if you don't get them written down. Later, of course, you will pray for the Holy Spirit's guidance in selecting which ones to use for your message.

For idea-catching, I use not note cards but a small digital voice recorder I carry in my shirt pocket. A voice recorder will make you a safer driver than note cards will! Make sure that you listen to the messages every night, though, so that they won't become victims of those strange electronic quirks that play havoc with microchips. Warning: once you start using a digital voice recorder, there's a good chance it'll become a necessity. I found this out when mine developed problems and I had to send it out of state for repair. It was like doing without part of my brain for a while!

Something else I carry with me is a lined pocket notebook and a pen or pencil. That way if I'm waiting for an appointment and have a few minutes, I can actually start outlining my sermon.

The Home Kit

- *Bibles.* As I've mentioned before, you'll need access to some literal translation Bibles, such as the King James Version, the New King James, the *New American Standard Bible,* and the English Standard Version. The Revised Standard Version is also good. The more contemporary, "playful" versions and paraphrases are fun to read—but make sure you study the literal ones first and most frequently. Your goal is to get as close as possible to what the original Bible writer actually said, without a modern spin added to it.

  Two vital points:

  First, no matter what version or versions you've used in your study, preach from the version that the people are most familiar with. If your church's pews have Bibles in the hymnal racks, use that version, so that unchurched, biblically illiterate visitors can follow easily along. If your congregation is "King

James Version only," don't inflict the otherwise delightful *Message* on them, or you'll rattle them so badly that they won't be able to focus on your main theme.

Second, never slander a Bible translation from the pulpit. I'll say more about this in just a few paragraphs, but never claim that one translation is "better" than another. Every day, the Lord is using missionaries' sincere if less than perfect translations to introduce salvation to people in foreign lands. If you announce that a particular version has flaws, you might turn someone away from the very Bible they'd become attached to and were reading devotedly.

This might be the place to take a closer look at—

Some Facts of Life About Bible Translations

When I was a kid, the King James Version (KJV) was the only Bible I knew. Even though the Revised Standard Version (RSV) was a decade or two old, most of the older people in my life regarded it with a certain amount of suspicion. Then, when I was in my 20s, the New International Version (NIV) came along, and young people embraced it with joy. The *New American Standard Bible* (NASB) arrived as well. About the same time, Kenneth Taylor provided us with his warmhearted *Living Bible* paraphrase (TLB).

Since then, of course, we've had many, many more.

How do we sort them all out? Which is best?

To start with, here are some ground rules to remember:

- *As I said, every Bible translation is a good one—if you understand why its editors translated it the way they did.* And the way to find out is to read the translators' introduction and whatever else you can find about the version. Kenneth Taylor's purpose was to paraphrase the Bible into language that his children could understand, and only later did others persuade him to publish what he'd written and call it *The Living Bible*. Most modern translators are trying to make the Bible readable by the average person, who might find older versions hard to concentrate on. Some versions even use a limited vocabulary, to attract readers whose first language may not be English.

- *It's important to keep in mind the difference between a translation and a paraphrase.* Scholars who create a Bible *translation* start directly from the original Hebrew (for the Old Testament) and Greek (for the New Testament). People who *paraphrase* the Bible, on the other hand, put it into their own words in the *same* language. That's what Kenneth Taylor did. He didn't begin with the original languages, but started with a literal English translation and simply rewrote it.

- *Every Bible translation can be positioned on a "more literal to less literal" line.* A bit later I'll show you a fascinating chart in which someone has done this. But first let's look at what some translations do with

῏Ην δὲ	ἄνθρωπος	ἐκ	τῶν	Φαρισα ων
Was but	man	from	the	Pharisees,

Νικ δημοs	ὄνομα	αὐτῷ,	ἄρχων	τῶν
Nicodemus	name	to him,	ruler	of the

᾽Ιουδαίων
Judeans.[1]

the same Bible verse.

To start with, here's John 3:1 in Greek, with a word-for-word English translation underneath each line:

Now, if we wanted a *really* literal translation of that, we could simply leave it word for word: "Was but man from the Pharisees, Nicodemus name to him, ruler of the Judeans." But neither you nor I nor most other readers would stand for verse after verse of that. Translators know that when they're transferring meaning from one language to another, they've got to be allowed a bit of wiggle room.

But some translators allow themselves a bit more freedom than others. *And again, that's OK,* if you know why they're doing it the way they are. The bottom line is that the translations that stay as close as possible to the original word order of the Greek or Hebrew are the *more literal* ones, while those that flex more are termed *less literal.*

Here are some examples of what I mean. I'll put the above word-for-word translation first, then give the King James Version (KJV), the New International Version (NIV), the New Century Version (NCV), and Eugene Peterson's *The Message* (Message).

word-for-word: was but man from the Pharisees

KJV: There was a man of the Pharisees,

NIV: Now there was a man of the Pharisees

NCV: There was a man [the "Pharisees" comes in the next phrase, below]

Message: There was a man of the Pharisee sect,

word-for-word: Nicodemus name to him,

KJV: named Nicodemus,

NIV: named Nicodemus,

NCV: named Nicodemus who was one of the Pharisees

Message: Nicodemus,

word-for-word: ruler of the Judeans.

KJV: a ruler of the Jews.

NIV: a member of the Jewish ruling council.

NCV: and an important Jewish leader.

Message: a prominent leader among the Jews.

Do you see what's happening? All those translations are saying basically the same thing—they're just using different words and phrasings. And again, that's OK, if you understand that some translators decide to do this more rigidly, and others more loosely.

Now let's look at the chart I promised you.

While I was working on this book, my wife, Shelley, discovered a real "find"—David Dewey's *A User's Guide to Bible Translations.*[2] If you're really interested in studying about both early and modern English Bible versions, this very readable book should answer most or maybe all of your questions.

In the following chart from page 76 of his book, Dewey does two things: 1. He carefully arranges 18 Bible translations on a "more literal" to "less literal" line. 2. He gives the grade-level readability of each of the versions.

Some quick definitions that will help you as you study the chart (I'll give you a list of the translations below the chart):

A form-driven version, according to Dewey, "is molded by the structure and style of the original language. Its aim is to come as close to the original as can be achieved in an English rendering."[3] In other words, form-driven versions try as much as possible to be word-for-word translations.

In a *meaning-driven version,* "the requirements of good, natural English determine the shape of the translation. A long Greek sentence may, for instance, be broken into several shorter English sentences. Word order may be rearranged."[4]

A *paraphrase,* of course, is rewriting a document in your own words, in the same language as some other translation.

On page 43 of his *User's Guide,* Dewey gives a delightful example of the three styles:

> *Form-driven:* "my cup overflows"
> *Meaning-driven:* "my life overflows with blessing"
> *Paraphrase:* "God blesses my socks off"

Now, let's have a look at Dewey's chart.[5] Afterward I'll tell you the full names of the translations.

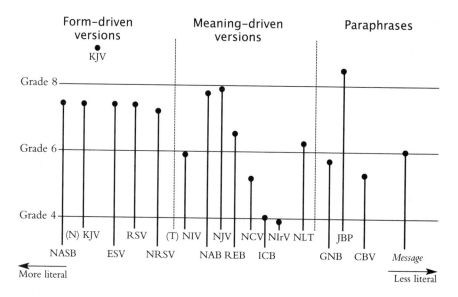

And here are the translations:

NASB	*New American Standard Bible*
KJV	King James Version (aka the Authorized Version) (1611)
NKJV	New King James Version (1982)
ESV	English Standard Version (2001)
RSV	Revised Standard Version (1952)
NRSV	New Revised Standard Version (1990)
TNIV	Today's New International Version (2005)
NAB	*New American Bible* (1970)

NJB	*New Jerusalem Bible* (1985)
REB	*Revised English Bible* (1989)
NCV	New Century Version (1991)
ICB	*International Children's Bible* (1986)
NIrV	New International Readers Version (1994-1998)
NLT	New Living Translation (1996, rev. 2004)
GNB	*Good News Bible* (aka Today's English Version) (1976)
JBP	J. B. Phillips' New Testament in Modern English (1958, rev. 1972)
CBV	[Dewey probably means CPV, the Cotton Patch Version] (1968)
Message	*The Message,* by Eugene Peterson

Now, one more ground rule, to which all the above has been leading:

- *It's safer to preach from a literal translation than a loose one.* Why? Because every preacher puts his or her spin on the message—and if you employ an already-spun translation, that *doubles* the spin.

So what's wrong with that? Let's say you're going in for heart-bypass surgery tomorrow. But this afternoon you discover that your doctor has learned most of his operating skills from a big fat suspense novel set in a hospital. Sure, the person who wrote the novel might be an MD, but wouldn't you feel a lot safer if your doctor had studied real medical text-books instead? That's an extreme example, but you get my point, right? For many parts of the Bible—such as Paul's writings—a literal translation is very, very important.

- *Late-breaking news!* Christmas happened while I was writing this book, and using a Christian bookstore gift certificate Shelley gave me, I purchased what will *definitely* be a very valuable tool for you. It's *The Evangelical Parallel New Testament,* and it's a side-by-side comparison of eight popular modern translations: the New King James Version, the NIV, the English Standard Version, the *Holman Christian Standard Bible,* Today's New International Version, the New Living Translation, the New Century Version, and *The Message.* It's published by Oxford University Press.

This book is actually the second in a series. You might also want to pick up the first one, *The Precise Parallel New Testament* (Oxford University Press). This edition (which I also own) has not only the Greek text, but also the King James Version, the *New American Standard Bible,* the NIV, the

Amplified Bible, Rheims New Testament, the *New American Bible,* and the New Revised Standard Version.

However, here's an important warning. (Highlight this paragraph.) Do *not* fall into the habit of quoting from several versions as you go along—like this: "The King James Version says that Nicodemus was 'a ruler of the Jews,' but the NIV says he was 'a member of the Jewish ruling council.' However, the NCV says he was 'an important Jewish leader,' and *The Message* calls him 'a prominent leader.'"

It's OK to do that once or twice in a sermon if you need to emphasize an important point. But any more of that, and you'll make your hearers really dizzy and disgusted. Preach from *one* version, not two or eight!

The Home Kit (Continued)

(In the appendix of this book I've included a larger list of study tools.)
* *Reference works. Don't use commentaries while you're working through this layperson's guide.* Your Christian bookstore will have loads of fat volumes on the books of Isaiah, or John, or Romans. Don't buy them—yet. (And don't wander into the bookstore and peek at the part that discusses the chapter you're preaching on! Thou shalt not steal!)

Why am I so serious about avoiding commentaries for now? Here's why. Not too long ago I preached on John 20. In order to create my sermon outline, I had to think and pray and scrawl my way through 18 notebook pages. In those pages I changed my outline twice before it satisfied me.

Let's say that after page 5 I'd given up and hurried to a commentary on John and read everything it had to say about chapter 20. If I had allowed my eye to scan those well-polished insights, I would have glanced back through my first feeble five pages and said, "Hey, what's the use? I might as well dump my own ideas and use an expert's instead!"

But I didn't do that. Instead I ignored the commentaries and plowed right through to notebook page 18. And now I have an outline that came from my own heart, my own study, not from the heart or the study of the commentary writer. And I can preach my own John 20 sermon with a whole lot more fervor than I could the commentary writer's.

Don't get me wrong. Commentaries can be helpful—*but don't use them yet.* This layperson's guide to expository preaching wants you to wrestle with the Bible text yourself.

But I'm not leaving you totally high and dry. Here are some other study tools that will fill in your knowledge gaps without stifling your creativity.

- *A concordance.* Let's say the chapter you've chosen to preach on has some material about child-raising, and you'd also like to mention the Proverbs verse that states, "Train up a child in the way he should go." A concordance (which alphabetically lists all the words in the Bible and the verses in which they are found) will bring you right to the passage you want. To find it most quickly, look up the least-common word in the verse, "train," and there it is: Proverbs 22:6.

  Or let's say you're preaching on Matthew 18, in which Jesus tells Peter to forgive 70 times seven. Even though your expository message will be based on that chapter, you also want to discover other things Jesus said about forgiveness. Take your concordance and look up the words "forgive" and "forgiveness" in Matthew, Mark, Luke, and John.

  If you spend a lot of time in the King James or New King James versions, *Strong's Concordance* is the best one to get, especially in the large font "comfort print" edition. You will also find a *New American Standard Bible* concordance (and a RSV one, and an NIV one, and some others). A good Bible computer software program will allow you to do the same thing that a concordance does. In fact, it's possible to download free Bible programs from the Internet, such as those at www.e-sword.net.

- *A Bible dictionary.* Check with your pastor or an experienced Christian bookstore salesperson for guidance on this. Since you're reading this book, the chances are that you believe—as I do—that when the Bible reports history, it's telling the facts. However, some theologians believe that several of the Bible's stories are ancient myths, so their comments might not be as useful to you. In general, a Bible dictionary contributed to by many different people from many different denominations (Baptist as well as Presbyterian, Nazarene as well as Episcopal) will give you a more balanced view.

  The Bible dictionary I go to the most often—and unfortunately it's a bit expensive—is the four-volume *International Standard Bible Encyclopedia,* affectionately known as "Izzbee" (ISBE). ISBE is published by Eerdmans, and the editors and the scores of Bible scholars who prepared it take the Bible very seriously. If there's any chance that you can muster up the cash for this set, it'll be a tool that you and your family will treasure for years to come.

  Also published by Eerdmans is a one-volume Bible dictionary: *Eerdmans Dictionary of the Bible.* It has a 2000 copyright date, so will include much material discovered since the publication of the ISBE.

- *Study Bibles.* Remember my warning to avoid commentaries for now? I feel slightly more friendly toward study Bibles—even though they too can seduce you away from doing your own careful "just you and the Word" study. Study Bibles do contain commentary (in the footnotes), but often it's more carefully written, since space is at a premium.

Warning: when you photocopy your Bible chapter for study, don't use a study Bible, because unless you cut them out, those seductive footnotes will travel right along with the chapter, and you'll be tempted to ignore your own serious study and peek down at them. *You'll discover much more than you ever thought possible by just spending time with the Bible passage itself.*

However, a good study Bible performs a valuable service, once you've fully developed your SPICATs. Since no one person can be a total expert on all of Scripture, a study Bible—and this is also true of a good commentary—can correct weird ideas you might come up with. Several times during my 23 years of expository sermon preparation I've had to eliminate a carefully plotted SPICAT because a study Bible's footnotes referred me to texts that proved I was dead wrong. But I rarely look at a study Bible's notes until I've created my SPICATs. I don't want to get dependent on someone else's thinking.

Right now I use only two study Bibles—the *NIV Study Bible* and the *Thompson Chain Reference Bible.* I think you should add them both to your library. *Thompson Chain* comes in several version—KJV, NKJV, NASB, NIV, and maybe others.

A warning as you check out other study Bibles: make sure they were prepared not by an individual but by a committee of people from many different denominations. Frank Thompson was an individual, of course, but he not only spent 40 solid years working on his *Chain Reference Bible*—he was also careful not to speculate about things the Bible isn't clear on. Sadly, other individuals who create study Bibles aren't always so conscientious.

Also, it would be best if the committee who prepared the study Bible that you're looking at came from those denominations who take the Bible literally. That's the case with the *NIV Study Bible.*

And every time you open a study Bible, always remember—the footnotes are *not* inspired. The Bible *is.*

See the Appendix for a List of Bible Tools

In the appendix at the end of this book I've included a more complete list of books and software I use while preparing a sermon. You might want to check it out.

Now we're ready to talk about—

How to Find and Use Good Illustrations

Right away you'll need to start stockpiling a good collection of illustrations. (Remember the humble "flashlight" sermon that stayed in the woman's mind after all the messages by all the pulpit greats had evaporated?) For your first sermon alone you'll need at least four appropriate illustrations—one for the introduction and one for each of the SPICATs.

First, a golden illustration rule:

- *The best illustrations are the ones you discover from your own past and present.*

Second, a no-no:

- *Don't collect and use sermon illustration books.* Not yet anyway. You can get dependent on them—and you never know which of those stories actually happened or which ones people have already heard. After all, Jesus didn't use sermon illustration compilations. The rabbis of His time told a lot of fables and parables, but the only time Jesus used theirs was to twist them back into truth!

Of course, it's OK to use illustrations from your general reading. If you enjoy looking through automotive or astronomy or golfing or sports magazines—or books on parenting or crafts or science or biography or any other subject—stay alert for usable material.

Here are some other ways to collect good, fresh illustrations and put them to use.

- *Keep your eyes—and all your other senses—open.* One night while driving home from a late church meeting, I smelled bread baking. I've enjoyed that delicious aroma many evenings since, and eventually I used the experience in a sermon. The nice thing about using a current illustration is that other people, driving on that same road by that same bakery, will smell that bread and—hopefully—remember the sermon truth it illustrated.

Another time I was in a huge warehouse hardware store. I heard a chirping sound, and looked down an empty aisle and saw three little birds huddled together on the floor. In that week's sermon I told about how we are like those birds, trapped in a sinful world far different from the Eden that God designed for us. Right now, there's no way out, but we can gain comfort from gathering together with others like us, until Someone tears off the roof and sets us free.

Last month, stopped in a long freeway backup, I happened to glance at the concrete barriers between the lanes. To my horror, I saw several long scrape marks on them. I haven't used this in a sermon yet, but when I do, I'll mention how those barriers are like God's Ten Commandments, which provide boundaries to keep us safe in a fast-moving and dangerous world.

People appreciate this kind of illustration because it's from today, not 60 or 100 years ago. Not too long ago I mentioned the message on a reader-board sign next to a local feed store, and after the sermon a man came up to me with his eyes shining. "I *know* that store," he said excitedly. "I *saw* that sign this week!"

I'm not saying that all my illustrations are as memorable as the flashlight with the little piece of paper in it. But at least they're fresh and recent, and people listen to them and have told me they appreciate them.

- *Have some way to record illustrations on the fly.* If you don't, you'll either not remember the illustration entirely, or you'll forget how you thought you could use it.

For years I've carried a mini-cassette recorder (and more recently a digital voice recorder) in my shirt pocket. Digital is best, because if you get the right kind, you can download the messages to your computer and listen to them on its speakers. You'll find it handy for other things, too, such as taking down to-do reminders to yourself, or directions to someone's house, or a great interview or Christian song on the radio.

If you go the note card route, you could rubber-band a batch of them together and keep them in your pocket or purse. At the next stoplight, grab the packet, scrawl a few notes on the top card, then slip that card underneath so you'll have a fresh one ready.

- *Do **not** limit your search to illustrations for the sermon you're currently working on.* I've found it's much better just to stay alert and notice anything that's funny, interesting, heart-touching, thought-provoking, or just plain wild, even though you may not immediately know how to use it.

For example, a couple months ago I was at a stoplight about a mile from our house. Hearing a loud cawing, I glanced left. There on the roof of a video rental store I saw two crows. One of them had a piece of food in its mouth, and the other was screaming. The first crow was trying to eat the food, but the other crow kept cawing in its ear. Finally the first crow gave up and let the other crow have a bite. I later used it in a sermon, making the point that God is *not* like the crow with the food—we don't have to scream at Him and pester Him before He'll listen and respond.

- *Don't immediately assign a "moral" to an illustration you find.* Sometimes I come across an illustration that perfectly illuminates a truth I'll be talking about in that week's sermon, so I'll note that point so I won't forget it. But even if the intriguing fact or scene or event I've noticed doesn't seem to have a moral, I make notes on it anyway.

  For example, I saw a life-size Superman statue in a Sharper Image store in a large city mall. Made of fiberglass, it had the blue suit, red cape, and all. I kept that illustration in my file for several months before I found a chance to use it in a sermon. Then I mentioned how we human beings have the foolish idea that we can be supermen and superwomen, solving our own problems and succeeding under our own power.

- *File your illustrations simply.* Want to hear about my "fancy" filing system? It's simply one long Microsoft Word document. Every time I find a new illustration, I add it to the *top* of the list. This document is 74 pages long so far, and it's so delightful, when I'm working on a sermon, just to page down through all those illustrations, starting at the top (I tend to favor recent illustrations rather than older ones). When I've used an illustration, I type "used" beside it, and transfer it to the bottom of the document. That way it's still available for other purposes, but it doesn't get tangled up in the newer ones. (One of my book evaluators suggested writing down when and where you used the illustration, to remind you of which groups of people have heard it.)

  The main reason I keep all my illustrations in one long document is that I'm worried that if I filed a new one under a topic name, I might forget the topic and not be able to find it again. It's a whole lot easier to hit the page down key several times within a single document, or do a word search. You can employ whatever filing system you want, but just make sure you'll have easy access to all your illustrations when you need them.

- *Don't illustrate your sermons with stories about your family or other church members.* Two reasons for this: First, not everybody wants to be spotlighted like this, especially kids, who get teased enough as it is. Second—even though you get permission from a church member to tell a story about him or her, you'll tighten the stomachs of everybody else. *I'd better watch my step,* they'll say to themselves. *Next thing I know, I'll be hearing about myself from the pulpit!*

- *Do use stories from your own childhood—but don't make yourself the hero.* People love to hear stories about a speaker's growing-up years. It makes the person in the pulpit more human, more vulnerable. But never cast yourself in the role of the hero, the problem solver, the scorer of the winning touchdown, the rescuer of the drowning dog. The minute you put yourself in the hero's role, people will think you're bragging, and they'll turn you off like a light switch. Remember Proverbs 27:2: "Let another man praise you, and not your own mouth; a stranger, and not your own lips."

Instead, if you show up in the story at all, it should be as someone who made a mistake, or learned a painful truth, or observed someone *else* being a hero. You can't remember stories from your childhood, you say? In the next chapter I'll teach you a dynamic method for jogging your memory.

- *Vital! Tie your illustration clearly to the point you're trying to make.* More than once, after I've finished a sermon, a layperson has come up to me with a puzzled look, commenting, "I couldn't quite understand why you told that first story." A pastor friend has some advice for lay preachers: "Tell me your illustration's point. Don't assume I'll know what it was. Even the disciples didn't always get the point of Jesus' parables. What do you want me to take away from your illustration?"

For now, I'll leave you with something I mentioned back in chapter 2:

- *Don't tell me stories that never happened and pretend they're true.* Please.

How's your hunt for a preaching chapter going? If you're reading this book as you're actually preparing a sermon, you should start zeroing in on it pretty soon. But whether or not you've found your passage yet, in the next chapter I'll tell you what to do with it. And I'll introduce you to *clustering*, an exciting (and free!) idea-generating and memory-jogging tool.

But for now, here's a very important homework project.

Homework Project 3—Start Collecting Illustrations

Carry a notebook or some note cards (or the brand-new digital voice recorder you're planning to buy at the office supply store) with you, and keep all senses alert as you move through your day. Try to discover *five* illustrations by tomorrow night. Don't try to figure out what they'll illustrate—unless that's immediately clear. Just get them copied down or recorded so you can look them over later.

If You're Working on a Sermon Right Now

- *Keep praying* that the Lord will help you create an effective sermon.
- *Definitely lock in* on a Bible chapter to preach on.
- *Assemble and start to use* both sermon preparation kits described in this chapter.
- *Start collecting illustrations of all kinds*—not just for the sermon you're working on. Store them where you can get at them when you need them.

GROUP DISCUSSION STARTERS

Think back on sermons you heard while you were growing up. Do you remember any of the stories the pastor told? If so, about how old were you when you heard it? Why do you think that particular story stayed with you?

Have you chosen a Bible chapter to preach on? If so, briefly tell the group what it is, how you chose it, and why.

Ask a pastor to bring to the group several sermon preparation resources (books, software information, etc.), and talk about why he or she has found them helpful.

Spend a few minutes discussing where to find items for your sermon preparation kits. Maybe one group session could be a car pool ride to a used bookstore. *Warning! Don't buy commentaries! (Yet.)*

Think back over the day you've just been through. Try to come up with three illustrations that might be usable for a sermon someday. Tell the group about it, and if possible, mention a spiritual truth each illustration might help teach.

---

[1] I'm using as my source the *Nestle-Aland Greek New Testament (27th ed.), with GRAM-CORD,* found on the Libronix Digital Library System 2.1 (© 2000-2002, Libronix Corporation).

[2] David Dewey, *A User's Guide to Bible Translations: Making the Most of Different Versions* (Downers Grove, Ill.: InterVarsity Press, 2004).

[3] *Ibid.,* p. 34.

[4] *Ibid.,* pp. 34, 35.

[5] *Ibid.,* p. 76.

4

Chapter Outline:

The Quilt Story

A few weeks ago my wife, Shelley, and I visited at the bedside of a woman in her 90s, just before she died. Elsie was a veteran quilter, and on our bed we still have the quilt she made us years ago, a detailed design in perfectly coordinated colors.

As I was starting this chapter, I wondered, *Did Elsie complete her one hundredth quilt much more quickly than her first—or her tenth?* Maybe she had indeed learned to quilt a little bit faster, but I doubt that she rocketed through that hundredth quilt at breakneck speed. The opposite was probably true. Since she most likely had a target person in mind for each quilt, I'm sure she took special care and made sure she did it right.

Or take the friend of ours whose hobby is restoring old cars. As he starts work on his next project, does he hurry? Does he cut a lot of corners simply because he knows what he's doing? Probably not. Instead, he may even sand and polish more carefully than ever. After all, he loves those aged autos.

And if you're a golfer, do you make it through nine holes three times as quickly as you did in your beginner games? Granted, you probably don't hit as many balls into the woods as you used to, but now you're probably even more careful, planning each drive more intelligently and deliberately than you ever could before. You take time to savor the experience.

I'm sure you get the point, right? Earlier I've told you that I've prepared and preached more than 600 expository sermons from scratch. And you might be thinking, *These days I'll bet Maylan can whip out a sermon in no time at all.*

Wrong.

Just like a quilter and an antique car restorer and a golfer, I now approach my sermon projects less casually and more carefully. For me, each new Bible chapter is still a challenge—and maybe *more* of a challenge, because by now I've learned just how much I might miss if I move too quickly. Less than a month ago I tackled a Bible chapter that was incredibly difficult. The subject matter was very important, but I couldn't immediately find a sermon pattern in it. I had to wrestle with that passage the entire week before I found a way I could use it.

Actually, preaching *shouldn't* get any easier. In fact, I've reached the point at which I'm highly suspicious of the first outline I come up with, because the chances are that what popped to the surface so quickly might be surface thinking. Of course I make notes on that first outline, and maybe I'll use a bit of it later. And sometimes that first brain wave is a winner. But just to make sure, I always go back and study the chapter again. And again. And again.

The Only Greek Word You'll Learn in This Entire Book!

If you were in seminary, what we're going to talk about next would have a fancier name: "hermeneutics." And you'd be using a far thicker textbook than this one.

By the way, hermeneutics comes from the Greek word *hermeneuō* (hair-men-YOU-oh), which means "to interpret." One of the most fun-to-pronounce Greek words is μεθερμηνευόμενον (*methermeneuomenon,* which is pronounced "meth-air-men-you-OH-men-on"—say it smoothly, not jerkily). μεθερμηνευόμενον shows up in such verses as Matthew 1:23, and it means "which being interpreted is" or "which is translated."

And buried right in the middle of that delightful seven-syllable word is *hermeneuō* (it's the "hair-men-you-oh" part). So when you study a Bible passage to get it ready for a sermon, you're doing *hermeneutics*—in other words, you're finding out how to "interpret" or "translate" that passage into the life and the culture of your hearers.

And that's where the following golden guidelines come in. They are vital. Don't skip any of them. (Note to pastors: this isn't designed to be an exhaustive discussion on hermeneutics, of course—just the basics.)

Golden Guidelines for Bible Interpretation

* *Treat the Bible as what it is—the Word of God.* My mother and father grew up in the Wesleyan Methodist faith, with a high regard for the Bible. Mom and Dad were so serious about this that if they saw a Bible on a table with other books stacked on top of it, they lifted the other books off and put the Bible on top. These days I still get privately uneasy when I see someone place even a pen or pencil on top of a Bible.

  "All Scripture is given by inspiration of God," Paul says, "and is profitable for doctrine, for reproof, for correction, for instruction in righteousness, that the man of God may be complete, thoroughly equipped for every good work" (2 Tim. 3:16, 17).

  Your sermon, therefore, should deal reverently with your chapter. *That doesn't mean humorlessly,* because as I told you in chapter 1, careful sermon humor is OK. But always signal to your listeners that you have the highest regard for Scripture and that you are submitting your own reasoning to God's wisdom.

* *Assume that the Bible is reporting real history unless there's a good reason not to.* Take Abraham, for example. The book of Genesis talks about him as though he's a historical figure. It shows him journeying over real geography (Iraq to Palestine) and interacting with real cultures, such as Egypt's. Jesus and the apostles mention Abraham several times and consider him a real person. So should we.

  However, if you're preaching on the beasts of Daniel or Revelation, you're dealing with something different. Daniel and John themselves were real people, but the beasts they saw in vision probably weren't actual animals snorting around in giant heavenly cages munching celestial alfalfa. They were more likely pictorial parables (might we say heavenly animated political cartoons?) that God flashed into the prophets' minds to help them transmit the message more dramatically.

- ***Study every verse in its context.*** Did you know that no Bible writer ever numbered his chapters or verses? The psalms (not the verses but the psalms themselves) were probably numbered early on,[1] but not by their original writers. All the rest of the chapter numbering came along during the thirteenth century, and verse numbering didn't originate until the 1550s.[2]

Verse numbering, of course, makes it a whole lot easier to point people to a certain text you want them to focus their attention on.

1. But verse numbering also seems to make every text a little separate gem of complete, stand-alone Bible truth.

2. It would drive me bananas, for example, if the editors of this layperson's guide suddenly added verse numbers to each sentence I've written.

3. I'm doing my best to put truth into each of my sentences, but *come on!*

4. And let's say you decided to preach a textual sermon on the second point. Wouldn't you want to include more of the context? Because for one thing, in that "verse" I'm *not* talking about literal bananas! It's only by reading more of what I've written that you get a feel for my casual, informal writing style.

With Bible passages the safest thing to do is to eliminate the verse numbers mentally and read the whole chapter without them. In fact, if you have Bible software, transfer the chapter into your word processing program and go through and delete the numbers. I do this, and I also narrow the column so that the Bible passage is only three or four inches wide. That gives me large margins for making notes.

Let me give you a couple of Bible examples of why context is so desperately important.

At first glance Genesis 31:49 seems like a kindly, pious blessing between two people: "May the Lord watch between you and me when we are absent one from another." I've even seen that verse printed on gift items in Christian bookstores. But if you read the context, you see it's something quite different—it's an angry challenge from Laban to his son-in-law Jacob that God will be watching if Jacob tries to cheat him.

Another example is Nahum 2:4: "The chariots rage in the streets, they jostle one another in the broad roads; they seem like torches, they run like lightning." My library has a tiny 100-year-old Scripture handbook that earnestly informs me that this verse is a Bible prophecy about automobiles racing through streets with their headlights on. But if I read the whole book of Nahum, I see that it's nothing of the sort. That verse is about actual chariots, not Chevys!

If you devote yourself to expository preaching, of course, you won't have to worry much about studying verses in their context. You'll already be dealing with chapters the way their original authors wrote them, the safest approach by far.

- *Evaluate every Bible act or comment in the light of statements by the Trinity.* Remember, God didn't always approve of everything people did. Just because Satan's statements are in the Bible, that doesn't make them true. Or just because David gloated over his enemies and wanted to destroy them, that doesn't mean that we should do the same. Jesus has the last word: *"Love* your enemies" (Matt. 5:44).
- *Preach the plain truths, not the obscure ones.* Once in a while you'll be working your way through your chapter and you'll come upon an interesting—but quite irrelevant—idea. Don't follow rabbit trails like that. Instead, remember that when all is said and done, you'll be standing before a congregation that includes single moms, seniors with prostate trouble, a man with a family to feed who's just been given two weeks' notice and no severance package, and a schoolkid who's miserable because he's been bullied all week. All of them are sitting there, hoping—either consciously or subconsciously—for a word from the Lord. So find the essence—the center, the main point—of your chapter, and preach that. *Make sure you give people courage for the week ahead.*
- *Discover and preach God's "Bible-wide attitude" about your topic.* What do I mean by this? That other parts of the Bible support the concepts you're bringing out of your preaching chapter. Some examples:

    Jesus said to cut off your hand or foot or gouge out your eye if either made you sin, right? (See Matt. 18:8, 9.) But throughout the entire Bible we find no record of anyone ever following that command. Jesus intended His statement to be a dramatic and figurative warning, not a Bible-wide practical guideline.

    Paul said that women shouldn't teach, but remain silent in church, right? (See 1 Tim. 2:11, 12; 1 Cor. 14:34.) But the rest of the Bible contains plenty of examples of women teaching and occupying important positions—Miriam leading the song of triumph after the Red Sea crossing, Deborah judging Israel, Huldah relaying the Word of God to the nation's leaders, Esther interceding for the Jews before the king, Anna prophesying about the baby Jesus, the evangelist Philip's four daughters prophesying (Acts 21), Lydia hosting a home church in Philippi. So Paul's advice must have been to a local situation, and not God's Bible-wide attitude. (Otherwise, who would teach our kids' Bible classes?)

To me, these are the major guidelines for Bible interpretation—at least those you need to remember right at the start.

However, there's one more tool I'd like to give you before we go any further. You need it now, because you're going to have to be generating illustrations and ideas and who knows what else.

Clustering

Clustering is also called mind mapping, bubble mapping, or spoking, and you might even be young enough to have learned it in school. And if you weren't taught it, your kids probably were, so get them to explain it to you at supper tonight! The principle is simple, and the more you use it, the more you'll like it. I'll explain it below, but if you like you can go to the library and check out *The Mind Map Book,* by Tony Buzan, or *Writing the Natural Way,* by Gabriele Rico. Or get online and search the words *mind mapping.*

Here's how I cluster. First, I get a sheet of copier paper, avoiding lined notebook paper because it tends to make me think I'm still hunched over an elementary school desk, which isn't a good mental posture for free-form idea generating. Then I adjust the paper *horizontally* on my desk, because again, placing it vertically makes me think *school* and tightens me up.

Let's say I'm trying to think of an event from my childhood that I can use to illustrate the concept of surprise. I draw a small circle in the center of the sheet and write "surprise" inside it. Then I start drawing spokes out from the circle. At the end of one spoke I write the name of the town I lived in as a child. At the end of another spoke I write "houses," and off "houses" I extend three other spokes, each representing one of the houses my family lived in. Off each house I'll draw a "backyard" spoke, a "my bedroom" spoke, a "kitchen" spoke, and so on. Then I'll draw another main spoke and label it "schools."

You can get as detailed as you want, but you probably won't have to.

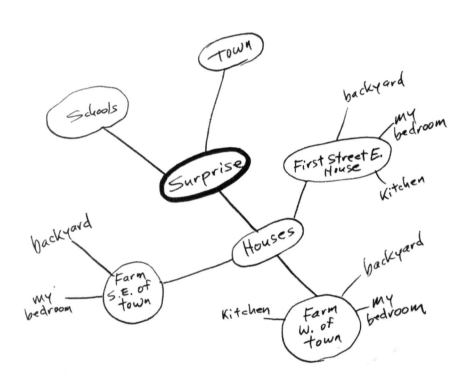

Example of Clustering

Because suddenly the magic happens—not supernatural magic, but the true magic of your God-created brain. Something will spark, and you'll remember some event or person that will be perfect for your illustrative needs. I once spent 20 unsuccessful minutes trying to think of an illustration with the usual scratch-my-head-and-stare-into-space method. Then I suddenly remembered clustering, and grabbed a sheet of paper and started drawing circles. And in less than 30 seconds I had exactly the illustration I needed.

What's the secret?

There's really no mystery about what's happening. You're simply freeing your brain to work efficiently. By simply writing down concepts or places (or whatever) on a sheet of paper, and drawing spokes, you're allowing your brain to relax and examine each option at its leisure rather than to have to juggle a whole jumble of ideas at the same time. As you've probably already figured out, the spoking is not only to connect the thoughts but also to make sure each new one has enough space around it so that you can add more details if you want to.

And clustering isn't merely an illustration generator. Use it to come up with ideas for sermon series, talks, articles, even books (in fact, I'm working off a humongous clustering chart as I write this layperson's guide). Use clustering with other people to plan your next church outreach project, or any other situation requiring immediate creative ideas. *As a pastor and writer, I consider clustering the most valuable tool I've discovered in the past 10 years.*

Happily, several software programs will let you do this on your computer screen. Simply do a search on *mind mapping software.* Make sure you check out several programs. Some may have downloadable trial versions. Try before you buy!

Tips for Taking General Notes on Your Preaching Chapter

Haven't chosen a chapter yet? Don't worry. I'll tell you what I did with one of mine, and you can use this information when you decide on your own. I call it taking "general notes," and it's a method I've employed for years with all my expository chapters. It's just a matter of getting so closely acquainted with your biblical chapter that you'll see some preaching patterns start to emerge.

Recently I preached on John 20. Here's how I handled it, and how I handle most chapters.

- *I photocopy or print out the chapter on a sheet or two of paper.* This makes my chapter a whole lot more convenient to carry around and study. Before I got computer Bible software I would photocopy the pages from the Bible, and then cut and paste so that I had only one column per page, and plenty of white space on either side of the passage to take notes on.

Now, since I have Bible software I copy the chapter into Microsoft Word, then make the column narrower to get the same effect. Normally I print out two English versions, and once in a while the Greek or Hebrew originals. I staple these sheets together, fold them with the print side out (so they'll stay open on a flat surface), and carry them around in one of those school composition notebooks I find in office supply stores. I like the wide-ruled (not college-ruled) notebooks the best, because that way I don't get fatigued from having to squeeze my words into a cramped space.

Note: You'll get a whole lot more out of what's below if you go get your Bible and open it to John 20. Read through the chapter before going any further here.

- *I start to read the chapter slowly.* Once again, *I am focusing on the chapter alone.* No commentaries, not even study Bible footnotes or concordances or anything, just the biblical material itself. Another thing to remember: at this point I don't yet know what my sermon's going to be about. I'm feeling my way along. A good part of the first series of notes I make probably won't even get used in the sermon.

- *I paraphrase the chapter.* In other words, I start putting it in my own words.

- *I start a "Sermon Title Possibilities" list.* Once in a while I'll come across a how-to-preach book that tells me not to give my sermon a title until I'm all done creating it. Don't you believe it! Even a tentative title can be a great way to focus thoughts. As I'm reading through my preaching chapters, titles will pop to mind. Often the early ones aren't any good. But sometimes they are.

- *If I find myself getting stuck, I ask the chapter three questions: "What?" "So what?" and "Now what?"* In other words, what does this chapter say to me, why is it important, and what do I do now that I know it?

An Example of How I Do General Notes

What follows are some of the actual general notes that I took on John 20. I'll put what I wrote in *italics*.

Possible title: "Reunion" or "Reunions."

Notice that I immediately started listing title ideas?

Because this is the chapter in which Jesus has risen and appears to Mary Magdalene and other disciples, "Reunion" seemed a promising idea. Here's my next general note:

*Stress the **happiness** in this chapter—the incredible joy people felt as they discovered that the ordinary, the routine, was now forever turned on its head.*

Then I began to list the reunions people had with Jesus in John 20: Mary Magdalene, the disciples, Thomas. Following that, I wrote:

*This chapter doesn't have a lot of doctrine—it's as though John is saying, "Rejoice with us!" This chapter is **story**.*

Later I added:

I wonder if the disciples were worried when they heard from Mary that Jesus had ascended? He was alive—but now He was gone to the Father. Whether He'd come back or not all depended on what He thought of the disciples.

Comment: The above paragraph probably isn't totally true, when you stop and think about it. But at this point, don't pause to examine the theological details of your general notes. Just capture every idea that comes along, and later you can prayerfully filter out the dubious ones. (As it turns out, I didn't even mention that paragraph in my sermon.)

As I continued to write in my notebook, I followed the "reunion" idea for a while, until I discovered it wasn't as strong as another idea that suddenly popped up. Here's what I was jotting down as the new idea dawned:

*Jesus could have stayed in heaven. But **Jesus returned!** Maybe that's the key to this sermon—"The **First** Second Coming." The first Second Coming happened Sunday evening.*

And that's what I ended up with as my idea. I called the sermon "The *First* Second Coming." We talk a lot about Jesus' second coming—and we're of course referring to His arrival in the clouds with angels. But what about His *first* second coming that Sunday afternoon? He rises from the dead and ascends to God, then returns to visit with His disciples that night. My points—which I later fleshed out into SPICATs—were these:

When Jesus returned that Sunday evening for His first second coming—

1. He showed up in person.
2. He brought peace.
3. He sent His disciples to do His most important work.
4. He treated doubters gently.

Each of those points—in true expository fashion—comes directly from the chapter itself. And as you can see, each of those points is also important for those of us who are waiting for Christ's *second* second coming.

You'll probably need several pages' worth of general notes before you hit on a pattern you can really preach. The John 20 sermon took 18 composition book pages (of large, scrawly handwriting) before I got the four points I listed above. A later sermon on John 21 took 27 notebook pages—and halfway through I switched the chapter to Luke 5!

"Hey, Maylan," I can hear someone say. "I'm the type who works things out in my head." OK, but make sure you get your thoughts down on paper at some point. It's often only when you write out your ideas that you can spot the weak parts.

Ready for some extremely important homework?

Homework Project 4—Photos of Your Listeners

If your church has a pictorial directory, copy photos of the following six people: (1) a single parent with kids; (2) an adult who's never been married; (3) an adult of a different ethnic background and skin color than yours; (4) a teenager who seems bored in church; (5) a 9-year-old boy or girl; and (6) a friend or coworker of yours who doesn't go to church. (If you can't get a picture of the friend, just write his or her name down on a piece of paper the size of the other photos.) Place the photos where you can see them as you prepare your sermons. This should help keep you from drifting too far into ivory-tower cloudland.

Homework Project 5—Your Three Favorite Pastors

Think back over your life. Who were your three favorite pastors? Take three pieces of paper and place one of the pastor's names at the top of each page. Then list (1) what was likable about each, and (2) what you remember about that person's preaching style.

If You're Working on a Sermon Right Now

- *Keep praying* about your sermon.
- *Read and study* your Bible passage in several literal translations. Start taking general notes.
- *Are you using* both the carry-along *and* the home sermon kits?
- *Are you gathering illustrations?* Try for at least five a day. Collect them now—evaluate them later.
- *Do some clustering* to discover illustrations from your childhood.

Discuss Homework Project 5. Give enough time so that each person has a chance to share.

Clustering: find out which person in the group feels most comfortable with clustering as described in this chapter. Ask that person to explain to the rest of the group step by step how to cluster. Then go on to the following in-class clustering exercises.

Clustering Exercise 1: Using pencil and paper, each person should cluster until he or she finds an actual event from childhood that illustrates the idea of repentance.

Clustering Exercise 2: Cluster the events of the past 24 hours, and discover as many potential illustrations as possible from them.

---

[1] Acts 13:33 mentions "the second Psalm."

[2] *The International Standard Bible Encyclopedia* (Grand Rapids: Eerdmans, 1979), vol. 1, p. 492.

5

Chapter Outline:

"Where Do I Begin?"

If you're a baby boomer, you remember that this was the first line of the song "Love Story." A love story, of course, is what you're creating as you work on a good expository sermon. And *where you begin* is indeed vital. Once more, take a look at these sermon elements:

The Classic Expository Sermon (A Review)

introduction

transition (which includes the "approach sentence")

SPICAT

SPICAT

SPICAT

one more SPICAT if absolutely necessary

conclusion/appeal

Assuming that you've chosen your preaching chapter, which of those elements do you think you'd need to work on first? Think carefully.

You may be surprised when I tell you it's the transition's "approach sentence." I'm going to define it in the following section—and I firmly believe that you can't do anything solid on your expository sermon until you get that sentence written.

Your Sermon's "Approach Sentence"

What do I mean by "approach sentence"?

On the Great Plains prairie where I come from, deep ditches separate highways from the adjoining fields. The ditches allow rainwater to drain away so the highways stay dry and the fields rarely flood.

Problem: how do you get your tractor or combine across those ditches and into the field to work your crops?

Solution: the "approach." You select a spot—generally close to a half-mile or mile mark—and you get somebody to haul in a lot of dirt and dump it into the ditch there (after first laying a large metal pipe known as a culvert to allow the water to continue flowing along). Once you pack the dirt down and smooth it out, it creates a narrow driveway—literally called an "approach"—over which you can drive your equipment into the field.

I like to think that the "approach sentence" allows each of your SPICATs—your fleshed-out sermon points—to travel from the sermon (the highway) across to your hearers (the field). Those SPICATs can be like farm machinery that plant, cultivate, and later harvest the crops—and the approach just makes it easier for the fields to receive the equipment. By the way, your listeners will be deeply encouraged when they hear your approach sentence, because it will send them the happy signal that a well-organized sermon is on the way.

Here's an example of an approach sentence from a sermon I preached last year. Notice that it consists of a single sentence.

Acts 26 provides us with several keys to "power witnessing."

See what I've done? In that sentence I've made you a promise: during my sermon I'm going to move through Acts 26 and tell you one by one what those power-witnessing keys are. I'm going to transport them over the "approach" driveway to you.

Here's an approach sentence I used in another sermon: *Ephesians 5 describes at least three "Christmas lights" that will brighten not only our holidays* but our hearts. Again, I've made a promise—to tell you what those "Christmas lights" are.

Here's another: *Exodus 16 describes four often-overlooked "manna miracles" that can increase our faith in a God who loves and cares for us.* "Aha," says the listener in the pew, "I get the strong feeling that this preacher is now going to go through Exodus 16 and tell me what those four miracles are."

Here are some other approach sentences from other sermons I've presented. Notice the words in **boldface,** because they're really important, and I'm going to talk about them in a moment.

*In Genesis 32, when Jacob "went to the mat" in a wrestling match with the angel, he learned three important **lessons.***

*Judges 4 challenges us to accept Deborah's three **"dares."***

*In 1 Kings 17 Elijah shows us three **steps** to becoming a "peak (mountaintop) partner" of God.*

*Psalm 139 suggests four **freedoms** we need to grant to God.* (I used it for a Fourth of July sermon.)

*Isaiah 6 and 7 provide us with several **steps** in a "sanctuary walk" that will show us how to play a central part in God's important plans.*

*Ezekiel 28 gives us a three-part "devil profile" **checklist** we can use to examine our own personalities so that we're not acting like the devil!*

*Mark 8 tells us about three **"gaps"** that need to be sparked if you and I are going to get our spiritual engines running smoothly.*

*John 12 shows how you and I are locked into several vicious **captivities,** but Jesus comes to liberate us from them.*

Do you see how the approach sentence works? It's simply an announcement to your listeners (and to yourself as you're working on the sermon) that you're going to deliver a well-focused series of truths from that chapter into their minds and hearts. As I said earlier, people brighten up when they hear such approach sentences—and they might even reach into their pocket or purse for a pen to take notes.

The Key Word

Did you notice that I **bolded** a word in each of the approach sentences above? Those words are examples of what Charles Koller in his book *Expository Preaching Without Notes* called the "key word." In my letter to pastors at the beginning of this book, I mentioned that Koller's was the first book on preaching I ever read. And his "key word" idea made such good sense to me that I've never forgotten it. A key word is a great idea focuser as you're writing your approach sentences and outlining your sermon.

The Internet tells me that what seems to be a more recent edition of Koller's book, called *How to Preach Without Notes,* was published in the late 1990s, so I'm not going to offer you his entire list of key words as I'd planned. But here are a few of them, from pages 53 and 54 of the 1979 printing, just to give you an idea. Once you see the principle, you'll just naturally come up with your own.

advantages	habits	realities
answers	incentives	reasons
arguments	insights	remedies
assurances	joys	risks
benefits	lessons	safeguards
blessings	methods	secrets
causes	obstacles	steps
challenges	perils	symptoms
conditions	principles	truths
dangers	problems	warnings
disciplines	questions	
examples	qualities	

There's gold in "that thar list," so right now while you're thinking about it, go to the inside back cover of this book and write "key word list" and this page number. You'll want to be able to find it easily as you work on your sermons.

As I mentioned, you don't have to stick with Koller's list. You can choose another key word, depending on the direction your sermon is taking. A few paragraphs back, my own approach sentence examples used some of Koller's words *(steps, lessons),* but also some that weren't on his list, such as *dares, freedoms, checklist,* and *gaps.*

So as you're working through your biblical chapter, writing your general notes and working on your approach sentence, keep this very valuable list handy. It might nudge you toward the perfect approach sentence.

What goes hand in hand with the approach sentence? The SPICAT— or more accurately, the "point" part of SPICAT. Again, the approach sentence signals that you're going to be introducing several points.

What's the Point?

Crack open a dozen preaching books and you'll probably find 12 different definitions, but they'll probably all be some variation of this:

A sermon point is a brief statement that clearly expresses a concept drawn from a Scripture passage, and which is linked by a central theme to other points from that passage to provide a progression of thought.

Let's break it down. Notice a few key words and phrases.

- *Brief.* Long, rambling sermon points don't stick in your hearers' minds.
- *Clearly expresses a concept.* Each sermon point should be easy enough for a 9-year-old to understand.
- *Linked to other points.* Your approach sentence, if carefully done, will express your main idea and keep your points linked together. But another kind of linkage is important too: grammatical parallelism. (More on this later.)
- *Progression of thought.* Your list of points shouldn't merely be a few interesting ideas strung together, but should help develop the main idea you're getting across.

How to Find and Polish Sermon Points

Oh, how I would like to give you a surefire recipe for coming up with sermon points. I've been preaching almost every week for 23 years, and it's still not easy.

But you know as well as I do that it *shouldn't* be easy. Art isn't easy. Picasso probably spent more energy on his later paintings than he did his first few. Brain surgery shouldn't be easy. Eye surgery shouldn't be easy. If I ever have my brain or my eye operated on, I would like to think that the surgeon wouldn't cut corners but would approach the task as though it were the most important surgical operation of the century. *Take me seriously, Doc.*

And that's what your Bible passage asks you to do. *Approach me seriously, Lay Preacher. Treat me reverently. The very mind of God pulses underneath my surface. So take care.*

Here are some guidelines to help you discover sermon points.

- *Study the "key words" a few pages back.* Also examine the boldface words in my sample approach sentences. The more you get a feel for what a key word and an approach sentence are, the better you'll be able to apply them to your Bible chapter.

- *See if your chapter naturally divides itself into sections.* A quick glance at Psalm 1 shows that it has two main sections: verses 1-3 talk about righteous people and the benefits they enjoy, and verses 4 and 5 discuss the wicked and their fate. Verse 6 is sort of a summary statement. You'd obviously have to do a lot more creative work on this to make it preachable, but at least you have a natural division to start with.

  Psalm 3 seems to fall naturally into three parts. Verses 1 and 2 mention that dangerous foes surround David, verses 3-6 announce how confident he is that the Lord is on his side, and verses 7 and 8 are a direct call to the Lord for help.

  Want a challenge? Take Daniel 9:1-19 and prepare a sermon called "How to Pray Daniel's Way." Your approach sentence could go something like this: "In the ninth chapter of his book Daniel models for us [number] steps to real intercessory prayer." Come up with three or four how-to steps as your points.

- *If you're having a hard time getting a grip on a topic, ask the chapter the following questions:*

  Who wrote this Bible chapter?

  To whom was it written?

  What do the chapter's original readers have in common with the people I'll be preaching to?

  Where is Jesus in this chapter?

  Where is the gospel in this chapter?

  If I were a nonbeliever and came across this chapter on a page ripped from the Bible and fluttering down the street, what would I find in it that might guide me toward God?

  If this chapter were the last one I ever read, how would it prepare me for a happy eternity?

  Does the chapter offer an example for me to follow?

  Does it point out errors for me to avoid?

  Does it outline any duties for me to perform?

  Does it contain any promises for me to claim?

  Does it demonstrate any prayers for me to echo?

  Once I read and understand this chapter, what are some ways I should behave differently come Monday morning?

Should You Use PowerPoint?

No doubt about it, presentation software such as PowerPoint is a powerful way to focus audience attention. However, I don't use it at all, and neither does my brother for the main body of his message. Chester, with the help of his wife, Cindy, will occasionally employ it for his conclusion/appeal segment. Cindy combines beautiful digital images with heart-touching songs, and their congregation leaves the service not only instructed by Chester's Bible preaching, but deeply moved by the appeal.

I'm going to suggest that you *not* use presentation software, at least for the main body of your sermons, and I'll give you a few reasons.

- *First, you have enough on your plate already.* You're learning a sermon style you've probably never preached before. As you're discovering how to do a good job of bringing forth Bible truth and translating it into today's terms, why add the headache of wrestling with software?

- *Second, presentation software tends to split your hearers' focus.* You need their attention on you. That's not ego—it's common sense. They need to see your facial expressions and your gestures. If you use presentation software, your hearers will end up staring almost totally at the screen, and you will become a radio broadcast that they listen to only part of the time. Remember, it's *you* who's doing the preaching, not the software!

- *Third, since you're modeling careful Bible reading and interpretation, why not have your hearers actually look at pages of real Bibles?* Once people discover that most of the Bible is pretty straightforward and easy to understand, they might just read more of it at home. But if all your texts are projected on a screen, your hearers will miss out on the hand-to-Book contact. Even if you tell them to follow along in their Bibles, that's merely splitting their attention even further. They'll probably just end up staring at the screen, Bibles unopened in their laps, waiting for the next slide to zoom or flicker or tumble into place.

"Doing without presentation software is a good idea in theory," one of my readers might be saying, "but in my church everything happens on-screen. We don't even *have* pew Bibles." If that's the case, why not type your preaching passage—and nothing else—into the presentation software, and project that onto the screen? Show the part of the verse you're talking about, then go to the next one. And insert blank screens when you want them to listen to you without distractions.

Homework Project 6—Decide on Your Preaching Chapter

OK, it's fish-or-cut-bait time. Decide on a chapter that you'll base your expository sermon on. Of course, if you're reading through this book just for interest's sake at this point, go ahead and read on. But if you're part of a group studying this book, or if you're already a lay preacher and your next sermon date is a month away, choose that chapter *now*.

If You're Working on a Sermon Right Now

- *Keep praying!* Say, "Lord, help me to find Your message, Your gospel, Your Son, in this chapter!"
- *Reread your Bible chapter.* Take more general notes. You're probably seeing some patterns develop. *Remember:* don't try to cram too much into your sermon! You do *not* have to cover an entire chapter!
- *Try out a few "approach sentences"* that naturally arise from the patterns you've discovered.
- *Develop points with these sentences.* Approach sentences and points go hand in hand—you can't have one without the other!
- *How many illustrations* have you captured so far? Don't stop collecting them! Look for them in unusual places. Watch people and animals. We often call nature "God's second Bible."

GROUP DISCUSSION STARTERS

Divide into groups of two, one person being the explainer and the other the listener. Without using this book, the explainer should present the concept of what an "approach sentence" is to the listener, and make up—or remember from the book chapter—a couple examples.

Each person in the group should give an example of a key word, and use it in a made-up (or real) sermon approach sentence.

Now for a mini-sermon outline drill. Everyone should sit in silence for 15 minutes. During that time each group member should read John 14:1-3 from his or her Bible, and come up with an approach sentence (including a key word), plus at least three points. When the time is up, group members should share their results.

6

Chapter Outline:

By now—if you're reading this book while preparing a sermon—I hope you're well into your Bible chapter, making all sorts of notes, and trying to come up with sermon points.

Want some more examples of points I've discovered in biblical chapters I've preached on? Below I've added sermon points to some of the approach sentences I listed in chapter 5. They are all real sermons I've preached in the past year or so. Again, I've **bolded** the key words.

Sample Approach Sentences and Sermon Points

*Approach: In Genesis 32, when Jacob "went to the mat" in a wrestling match with the angel, he learned three important **lessons**.*

Point 1: Jesus wrestles.

Point 2: Jesus wrestles to show me my strength.

Point 3: Jesus wrestles to bring me face to face with my human nature.

Approach: Judges 4 challenges us to accept Deborah's three **"dares."**
    Point 1: Dare to trash tradition to go with God.
    Point 2: Dare—because you and God are a majority.
    Point 3: Dare to believe that in God's battles, God goes first.

Approach: In 1 Kings 17 Elijah shows us three **lessons** to becoming a "peak (mountaintop) partner" of God.
    Point 1: Learn to fearlessly dare God's dares.
    Point 2: Learn to wait and trust.
    Point 3: Learn "hungry prayer."

Approach: Psalm 139 suggests four **freedoms** I need to grant to God.
    Point 1: The freedom to pay me full attention.
    Point 2: The freedom to be my Creator.
    Point 3: The freedom to arouse my anger against wickedness.
    Point 4: The freedom to search and destroy the evil in my heart.

Approach: Isaiah 6 and 7 provide us with several **steps** in a "sanctuary walk" that will show us how to play a central part in God's important plans.
    Point 1: We need to move mentally and emotionally into God's sanctuary.
    Point 2: We need to welcome God's presence wholeheartedly.
    Point 3: We need to say yes when God asks for encouragers.

Approach: Ezekiel 28 gives us a three-part "devil profile" **checklist** we can use to check our own behavior so that we're not acting like the adversary! You know you're "acting like the devil"—
    Point 1: When you say, "I want to be God."
    Point 2: When you take credit for gifts that God has given.
    Point 3: When you grow violent inside.

Approach: Mark 8 tells us about three **"gaps"** that need to be sparked if you and I are going to get our spiritual engines running smoothly.
    Point 1: The gap between impossibility and miracle.
    Point 2: The gap between pride and humility.
    Point 3: The gap between parable and point.

*Approach: John 12 shows how you and I are locked into several vicious **captivities**, but Jesus comes to liberate us from them.*
>   *Point 1: Jesus liberates us from sin's slavery.*
>   *Point 2: Jesus liberates us from death.*
>   *Point 3: Jesus liberates us from greed.*
>   *Point 4: Jesus liberates us from God-slander.*

More About Linking Your Points

Did you notice something about the points in my examples? By and large, they were *grammatically parallel.*

"Whoa," I can hear someone mutter. "Please don't tell me we're about to wade hip-deep into English 101."

Not at all. I'm *not* going to launch into a lecture about subjects and verbs and direct objects—just be aware that in order to make your points memorable, they'll need to be not only brief but have the same structure. For example, I preached a sermon earlier this year on John 9 called "Three Blindnesses." Here's the approach sentence and the points:

*Approach: John 9 tells us that as Christians we're in danger of being infected with three **blindnesses**, and we're in need of Jesus' healing.*
>   *Blindness 1: When we can't see beyond the propaganda to the Parent.*
>   *Blindness 2: When we can't see beyond the rules to the relationship.*
>   *Blindness 3: When we can't see beyond the persecution to the peace.*

Those points are *parallel*—they all start with "When we can't see beyond the," and each concludes with "_____ to the _____."

People deeply appreciate it when you take pains to make sermon points memorable. Remember, *you've* been working on your sermon for many hours. You've been living with those ideas, and you understand them pretty well. But your half-hour preaching event may be the first and only time the congregation hears those concepts, so do whatever you can to make sure they're clear. I always reserve a couple notebook pages just to write and rewrite my sermon points so they'll be parallel.

"But how can I get from the Bible chapter to a series of sermon points?" you might be asking.

Here's an incredibly useful—and incredibly free—tool.

Freewriting to the Rescue!

Have you ever noticed that if you're facing a problem, it's sometimes nice to just talk the issue through with a friend? And that's what freewriting is, except that in this case the "friend" is a piece of paper.

Freewriting is simply putting your pen or pencil on paper (or your fingers on the keyboard) and just composing a conversation to yourself. It's a way of breaking the logjam in your mind, a method of getting something moving. I can't tell you how many times it has started me in the right direction. Let me show you how it works.

Here's an actual example of some freewriting I did when I got stuck while preparing an expository sermon on Daniel 9. Opening my notebook, I picked up my pencil and wrote this:

I need an introduction . . .

So now what?

Daniel 9 tells us why we need Jesus.

But we need an intro. How do I find an intro? First I need a basic theme. What does Daniel 9 say about why we need Jesus?

Wait. Let's start with setting the stage. Describe Babylon. Or maybe Daniel wasn't in Babylon at that point.

Or maybe get more intimate. Have him in his house. Have him in his bedroom, where he has a window that opens toward Jerusalem. What are Daniel's emotions as he begins his prayer? He's afraid that the Lord might delay the return from captivity.

Daniel needs Jesus. He would probably not have defined the Messiah the way we do. Daniel needed the kind of Messiah who was a prince, a conqueror.

By now you're probably frowning in puzzlement. "Maylan isn't making a whole lot of sense," you say. "He's jumping all over the place and just seems to be feeling his way along."

Exactly. That's what freewriting is: feeling your way along, getting your brain moving, starting to explore some options. If talking is easier for you than writing, get in a room by yourself (or take a walk) and do free*talking*.

Warning. Even though I mentioned that freewriting is something like talking an issue through with a friend, it might be wise *not* to use a real friend to do this with. For one thing, your friend might shoot down good ideas that simply need time to mature and that will end up making your sermon really strong. For another thing, he or she might try (in a well-meaning way) to create a sermon outline for you—which means it won't be your sermon anymore.

Want more information on freewriting? Go online and search with the word "freewriting," and you'll find some most helpful material. (However, shy away from anything that sounds spooky, or tries to get you in touch with your "inner child." Remember, you're working on a sermon, not going through psychoanalysis!)

Alliteration Alert!

I might be stepping on a few toes in what I say next, so whoever wants to slip into steel-toed work boots may do so at this time.

Do you see the phrase "alliteration alert" above? That's an example of alliteration. Alliteration is two or more words close together starting with the same letter or sound. Such as "leapin' lizards"; "great guns"; "happy hunting."

Alliteration is a habit that a lot of preachers—lay and professional—have fallen into. You can see why they do it, of course. They want to make their sermons stick firmly in the mind, so that their listeners can think about them during the week ahead.

But things have gone too far, my friends. *Much too far.* I'm going to invent an example of what I've seen happening in sermon outlines I've noticed recently. (Thankfully, the following was never an actual sermon.)

> *Paul urges Christians to—*
> **Point 1:** *Do our Duty.*
> **Point 2:** *Double our Donations.*
> **Point 3:** *Demand Decisions.*
> **Point 4:** *Develop Disciples.*

Don't get me wrong. I'm not against a little alliteration from time to time. (Even I used it in the "blindness" sermon points a few paragraphs back—"propaganda/Parent," "rules/relationship," "persecution/peace.") But I just think it needs to be employed sparingly and judiciously, as with a tiny bottle of hot sauce on a restaurant table.

However, I've noticed that some people get so obsessed by alliteration that they seem to be spending a whole lot more time with a thesaurus than with theology. (Uh-oh. I alliterated "thesaurus" and "theology." Could alliteration be one of those pandemic diseases everybody's warning us about?)

Seriously, when I come across the outline for someone's awesomely alliterated sermon, I find myself wondering, *H'mmm. Could it be possible that our worthy alliterator may have slightly altered a Bible concept to make it fit the Delightful Drove of D's for which he or she has been Deftly Diving into the Desktop Dictionary?* Sure, the English language is a marvelous thing, containing hundreds of thousands more words than any other language, and the Potential Point Possibilities are Perfectly Paralyzing, but . . . ?

May I suggest a couple alliteration guidelines?

- ***Don't use it every time.*** If you condition your audience to expect alliteration in every sermon you preach, they might become so intrigued with what your next "T" phrase might be, especially if it's humorous, that they might miss the deep seriousness of your Bible passage.

- ***If you have to alliterate, do it in other parts of the sermon besides the points.*** I use alliteration quite a lot in my sermons, but I don't call attention to it. Remember a few paragraphs back when I mentioned spending more time with a *thesaurus* than with *theology?* That just came naturally off my tongue—or rather, my typing fingertips. Alliteration's OK, but just keep it in its place. Don't let it Dictate or Distort Divine Doctrine!

Just for Fun!

Now that I've vented about alliteration, here—just for the fun of it—is something a friend of mine forwarded to me recently. Maybe you've seen it already:

The Footloose Fugitive

Feeling footloose and frisky, a featherbrained fellow forced his father to fork over his farthings. Fast he flew to foreign fields and frittered his family's fortune, feasting fabulously with floozies and faithless friends. Flooded with flattery, he financed a full-fledged fling of "funny foam" and fast food.

Fleeced by his fellows in folly, facing famine, and feeling faintly fuzzy, he found himself a feed-flinger in a filthy foreign farmyard. Feeling frail and fairly famished, he fain would have filled his frame with foraged food from the fodder fragments. "Fooey," he figured, "my father's flunkies fare far fancier."

The frazzled fugitive fumed feverishly, facing the

facts. Finally, frustrated from failure and filled with foreboding (but following his finer feelings), he fled from the filthy foreign farmyard.

Far away in the field the father focused on the fretful familiar form, and flew to him and fondly flung his forearms around the fatigued fugitive. Falling at his father's feet, the fugitive floundered forlornly, "Father, I have flunked, and fruitlessly forfeited family favor."

Finally the faithful father, forbidding and forestalling further flinching, frantically flagged the flunkies to fetch forth the finest fatling and fix a feast. The father's faithful firstborn was in a fertile field fixing fences while father and fugitive were feeling festive. The farm foreman felt fantastic as he flashed the fortunate news of a familiar family face that had forsaken fatal foolishness.

Forty-four feet from the farmhouse the firstborn found a farmhand fixing a fatling. Frowning and finding fault, he found father and fumed, "Floozies and foam from frittered family funds, and you fix a feast following the fugitive's folderol?"

The firstborn's fury flashed, but fussing was futile. The frugal firstborn felt it was fitting to feel favored for his faithfulness and fidelity to family, father, and farm. In foolhardy fashion he faulted the father for failing to furnish a fatling and feast for his friends. His folly was not in feeling fit for feast and fatling for friends—rather his flaw was in his feeling about the fairness of the festival for the found fugitive. His fundamental fallacy was a fixation on favoritism, not forgiveness. Any focus on feeling favored will fester, and friction will force the faded facade to fall.

Frankly, the father felt the frigid firstborn's frugality of forgiveness was formidable and frightful. But the father's former faithful fortitude and fearless forbearance to forgive both fugitive and firstborn flourishes. The farsighted father figured, "Such fidelity is fine, but what forbids fervent festivity for the fugitive that is finally found? Unfurl the flags and finery; let fun and frolic freely flow. Former failure is forgotten, folly is forsaken. Forgiveness forms the foundation for future fortune."

Four facets of the Father's fathomless fondness for faltering fugitives are:

1. Forgiveness
2. Forever faithful friendship
3. Fadeless love, and
4. A facility for forgetting flaws

Did I say something about alliteration becoming pandemic? Somebody get on the phone to the Centers for Disease Control!

Write—and Speak—*Naturally!*

After I'd written this book, I farmed it out to several people to evaluate, one of them was an experienced pastor and trainer of pastors.

"Please," he urged me, "encourage your readers to give their sermons a conversational style."

He makes an excellent point. Haven't you heard sermons that sound more like scholarly articles, theology lectures, or book chapters? How do you avoid this problem?

The key is to remember that there's a world of difference between what's written for the eye and what's written for the ear. I've found this very true when I've tried to get some of my sermons published as articles. Each time I couldn't simply use the sermon "as is," but had to start over from scratch.

Here are some guidelines to keep in mind as you write for the ear and not the eye.

- *Your hearers have only once chance to understand your sermon.* They can't go back and reread a paragraph that puzzled them, nor can they replay it in their minds. "Ah," you might be saying, "but our audiovisual people tape the sermons. People can just get the recording, can't they?" The facts are that if you've befuddled the congregation at all, they're probably not going to take the trouble to get your tape. Simplify, simplify, simplify!

- *Your hearers have **less than one chance** to understand your sermon.* All around them are distractions—crying babies, older kids scuttling out to

79

the restroom and then barging back in, the moan of an ambulance siren on the street outside. Even a thought-provoking sermon comment, or story, can cause listeners to stop paying attention so they can process what they've just heard. So plan to leave breathing spaces between "big ideas." That's another reason the SPICAT format is so helpful—it builds in those breathing spaces, and gives people a user-friendly framework for processing what they hear.

- **Run down to the grocery store and buy the textbook!** I'm not kidding. Any popular magazine will give you examples of user-friendly writing. Even though *Reader's Digest* has been shouldered aside on some magazine racks by more picture-oriented publications such as *People,* the *Digest* is still a world-class example of how to write for both ear and eye at the same time. Buy a copy and read several articles out loud to see how they do it.

In the next few paragraphs I'm going to show you how I changed a rather dull piece of writing into something more cheerful and "ear-friendly." A moment ago I went to my bookshelf, grabbed a sober and scholarly book, and opened it to a paragraph in which the author was quoting church historian Kenneth Scott Latourette, who lived and wrote about a century ago. To be fair, Latourette was writing a history chapter for the eye, not a sermon for the ear.

But sadly, a number of inexperienced preachers produce boring material something like this, and assume the congregation's going to be interested in it:

> *Written for the eye:*
>
> "Christianity, by bringing the church into existence, developed an institution which in part was a rival of the state. It created a society within the empire which, so many believed, threatened the very existence of the latter. . . . When Constantine made his peace with the faith, however, it long looked as though the conflict had been resolved by the control of the church by the state."

Pretty dry, right? If someone paid you $500 to get up and read the entire chapter that paragraph came from, word for word, and make it interesting, you'd have to pull out all your acting skills, dramatic voice variation, striking gestures, PowerPoint programs, and laser pointers to put some life into it. And even then people would get weary after two or three pages. That material is simply too dense, too tightly packed with ideas, too lacking in illustrations.

Now let's pretend that the Christian history paragraph above wasn't from a book, but was part of the first draft of a sermon I was writing. Here's how I would change it to make it more ear-friendly:

Rewritten for the ear:

"Let's pretend that you and I go downtown and stand on the corner of Main and Seventh. We're gripping clipboards in our fists, and clamped to those clipboards is a piece of paper with only one question on it. While people stand waiting for the 'Walk' sign, we grab them by the shoulders and ask them the following question:

" 'On a scale of 1 to 10, with 1 being harmless and 10 being dangerous, how would you rank the Presbyterian (or Nazarene, or Methodist, or whatever) church down the street there? Is it dangerous, or harmless, or somewhere in between?'

"Chances are, most people would chuckle, and rate it a 1, or at most 2 or possibly 3.

"But it was exactly the opposite when Christianity began. If we'd have stood on a street corner in first-century Rome and asked that question, we would have gotten 8s and 9s and 10s. Because the Roman Empire felt really threatened by the church.

"Looking at it with twenty-first-century eyes, we can't imagine why they got so flustered. But when you think of it, when the Christian church came along it actually turned out to be something like a rival to the state. It was its own little society, within the larger empire. And this made the emperor very uneasy, because something about that little society threatened his power.

"But then, along came the emperor Constantine, and things changed. Under his guidance, the state got so that it actually *controlled* the church. And for a while people thought that was fine."

Do you see what happened when I rewrote the boring paragraph? As I moved the action into the twenty-first century, I had to use a lot more words. That's because I not only had to leave more breathing room, but also had to relate it to real life. So if your own sermon's first draft sounds more like the boring paragraph, breathe some life into it. Pretend that you're talking about your topic with someone during a break at racquetball practice. Be enthusiastic, and it'll rub off on your hearers.

Shall I Do a Full Manuscript? Partial Manuscript? Outline?

When you finally stand behind the pulpit and take that first breath, what kind of sermon notes do you hope to be looking at?

Do you want everything written out, word for word? If so, you'll be preparing a *full manuscript*. Should you prefer to "tell" part of the sermon, but write out the parts that you want to get exactly right, you'll be working with a *partial manuscript*. And if your notes are simply made up of words and phrases to jog your memory, you're using an *outline*.

Which format should you use? Let's look at some pluses and minuses of each one.

- *The full manuscript.* I'll tell you right up front that this is the plan I've been using for more than 20 years. And a number of preaching books strongly urge beginners to write out their first several sermons word for word.

Some pluses. With a full manuscript, you get the chance to polish your ideas and link them together in the privacy of your own study. You'll know before you step into the pulpit exactly what you're going to say. A full manuscript is the perfect way to squelch "uhhhh's" and other speech mannerisms. Not too long ago I listened to the tape of a speaker who said "Wow!" about every fourth sentence, which got to be pretty tiring.

Another common habit that speakers fall into is repeating themselves. "King David just *loved* to praise the Lord. [pause] Just *loved* to praise the Lord." Some people do this quite unconsciously, probably to stall for time while they're thinking of what to say next. A full manuscript will eliminate repetitions that you don't intend.

Another full-manuscript plus: you can post your sermon on a blog or a Web site in case you need to. What's more, if you ever have to preach somewhere else, you can pull the manuscript out of your files and know exactly what you're going to say—or you can pull it up on the computer monitor and revise it.

Some minuses. If you don't know how to type, or don't do it quickly, preparing a full manuscript will be pretty irksome. (However, voice recognition software has advanced so much that it's breathtakingly easy to dictate your words into a headset and watch them appear on the monitor! See the "Some Resources I've Found Helpful" section in the appendix.) Another minus is that you'll need to be willing to tweak and rehearse your message onscreen until it comes across like talking and not writing. Still, this is excellent practice for a beginner. I'll go along with the preaching books and urge you to follow the manuscript route if you can, for at least the first two or three expository sermons you preach.

- **The partial manuscript.** This is next-best to the full manuscript, and you might find it a better route, especially if you've had some experience in public speaking or if you don't think you could make a full manuscript interesting.

  With the partial-manuscript format, you write out word for word only certain parts of the sermon. My strong suggestions would be to prepare fully the sermon's introduction, the transition (including the approach sentence), the "point" and "transition" parts of your SPICATs, and finally your conclusion/appeal. Carefully outline the rest.

  Pluses. You save time with the partial manuscript, yet you'll have the main parts of your sermon secure. And you'll experience greater freedom in speaking.

  Minus. You'll have to rehearse differently than you would with a full manuscript. Since your outlined sections are more sketchy, you'll need to make sure before you enter the pulpit that you can deliver them clearly and without fumbling (or repeating yourself).

- **The outline.** The only times I use outlines these days is if I'm teaching something. If I ever do seminars on this book, I'll work from an outline, not a manuscript.

  Pluses. An outline is great if you know your material very well and have rehearsed it very thoroughly (or have presented it many times before). You can also easily add notes in pen or pencil in case you think of new illustrations or ideas.

  Minuses. One of the reasons I stopped using outlines years ago (at Shelley's suggestion) was that I would preach them too rapidly. Often I would overprepare, and it would mean that I would have to rush to get all my material in. Also, to preach an outline well you need more rehearsal time than the two previous styles. If you use an outline, ask your spouse or someone else for his or her candid feedback on how well you use this approach.

Let's take a chapter break. Here's another valuable homework assignment.

Homework Project 7—Take General Notes on Your Chapter

Move prayerfully through your selected sermon chapter and jot down general notes. Just write down ideas that come to mind—possible sermon titles, possible approach sentences, possible points, possible illustrations.

If You're Working on a Sermon Right Now

- *Keep praying!* Say, "Lord, help me to find Your message, Your gospel, Your Son, in my chapter!"
- *Spend some time making your points parallel* in form. If you have discovered more than four points, consider dropping the weakest, or combining it with the point next to it. Or you can always save it (and strengthen it) for a devotional talk.
- *Develop a wary attitude toward alliteration!* Don't let it get you by the throat!
- *As you compose your sermon, write for the ear!*

GROUP DISCUSSION STARTERS

Read your general notes on your sermon chapter aloud to the group.

During five (or more) minutes of silence, all group members should write out a one-sentence description of what their sermons are about. Those who aren't quite sure of this yet should prepare a sentence about what they *hope* their sermon will be about. Each person should read his or her sentence to the group.

Here's an exercise in speaking naturally. Group members open their Bibles and hunt for a favorite verse, and mentally "translate" that verse into casual conversational style. (Pencil and paper may be used if needed.) They first read the original Bible verse aloud, then its twenty-first-century "translation."

Divide into teams of two. Without looking at this chapter, each team member should explain to the other the manuscript style (full manuscript, partial manuscript, or outline) that he or she is tentatively planning to use for the sermon being worked on, giving as many reasons as possible for the choice.

Group members should have opportunities to share difficulties they may be struggling with as they construct their sermons. Suggestions and encouragement should be exchanged.

7

Chapter Outline:

N ow, while you're busily making general notes and crystallizing your approach sentence and your sermon points, let's consider the very important matter of—

The Sermon Time Line

Every once in a while you'll hear preachers—generally inexperienced ones—give really long and embellished introductions. When they finally get to the body of the sermon, they either have to rush madly through it or simply beg the congregation's permission to run overtime to get everything in.

Which reminds me of a sermonic golden rule: *Don't ever mention the time.* Shelley introduced me to this rule, and it's an excellent one. The average congregation becomes four times as time-conscious (and four times as antsy) once the speaker mentions the time or even glances at a wristwatch.

One way to avoid time problems is the sermon time line. The one I'm suggesting below is only a rough guideline. It's based on the idea that the SPICATs are a sermon's most important parts. I believe that the SPICATs should receive the most time, and fairly equal time among themselves. I did a word count of my most recent sermon, and here's a percentage breakdown according to how much time I spent on each segment.

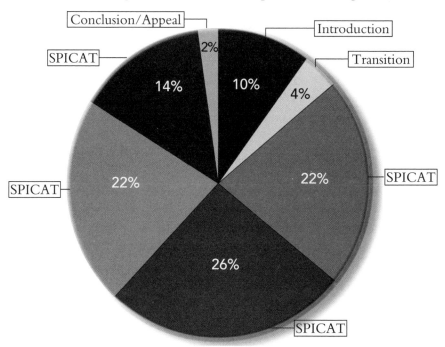

That's a good general rule to follow. Your introduction shouldn't take up any more than 10 percent of the total—and ideally a bit less. Your transition should be quick, and each of your SPICATs should take up roughly the same amount of time. Your conclusion/appeal should maybe be a bit longer than my 2 percent above. (Again, your congregation's culture should guide you here—especially if they're used to longish appeals or altar calls.)

Remember, a total of 30 minutes or less is your goal. (If your culture allows for longer sermons, carefully expand times, but keep them proportional.) Here's how the above sermon might break down into minute lengths, based on a 30-minute total.

	Minutes
Introduction	3
Transition	1
SPICAT 1	6
SPICAT 2	8
SPICAT 3	6
SPICAT 4	5
Conclusion/Appeal	1
	30

Some hints. As I mentioned earlier, make sure you keep a strong grip on your introduction, because if it spills over into your SPICAT time, you—and your listeners—will feel the pressure. The transition to your first SPICAT need not be long. As I mentioned, your conclusion can be longer than mine was in the sermon above, but you'll have to slice a bit off your SPICATs to keep everything within the 30-minute range. (In the next section I give a couple suggestions about how to clock your sermon length.) The time you have for your SPICATs, of course, depends on how many you include. The four SPICATs above total 25 minutes. So if you have two, that equals about 12 minutes apiece. Three would mean you'd spend about 8 minutes on each one.

Why do I keep insisting on the 30-minute rule? I think that—unless a congregation is strongly conditioned to listen to longer messages—the sermon-hearing mind starts to go numb after the first half hour. Staying within 30 minutes is good discipline, too, and leads to many repeat speaking opportunities.

And remember, if you find you're overtime during rehearsal, cut out the least-important SPICAT. *Eliminating a SPICAT is better than trying to downsize it along with the others—because downsized SPICATs often become too thin.* Save those leftovers, though. You might be able to use them later as individual devotional talks, or as parts of topical sermons.

How to Time Your Sermon

- *The word count method of timing.* If you write your sermons out word for word, as I do, timing is easy. Simply use the guideline many radio and TV broadcasters employ: 150 words equals one minute. That means that a 30-minute sermon, delivered at a normal rate of speaking without unusual pauses, would be 4,500 words long.

How do you count the words? Microsoft Word has an automatic word count feature: Hold down the alt key and tap T, then take your finger off alt and tap W. I'm pretty good at keeping my sermons between 3,500 and 4,000 words. (Last weekend's message, for example, was 3,650.)

Important note: As you're clocking your sermon, make sure that you include the time it takes to read aloud the Scripture segments you'll be quoting. Since I post my sermons on my church Web site, I make a habit of loading each Scripture passage completely into the manuscript as I write it, which means I can also keep a dependable running word count. But when I preach the sermon from the pulpit, I read the scriptures not from the manuscript but from my open Bible, which I hold in my hand so that my hearers can see it.

- *The rehearsal method of timing.* If you preach from an outline rather than a manuscript, you'll need to time yourself as you practice. To make this easier, you might want to go down to a sports store and buy a stopwatch.

A Sample Sermon Segment: Introduction, Transition, and One SPICAT

What I'm going to do now is to print out the actual manuscript of the first part of one of my recent sermons: the introduction, the transition, and the first SPICAT. *In bold, italicized print I'll comment on what's happening as we go along.*

Points or Paths?
Expository Sermon on Proverbs 4

MAYLAN TO READER: I preached this sermon on the occasion of the baptism of a teenage boy whom I'll call Mark, which isn't his real name. I always ask baptismal candidates to choose a scripture for me to preach on. But rather than just using the verse or two they provide, I'll often do an expository sermon on a larger segment in the chapter—making sure to include their chosen verses, of course.

Please open your Bibles to Proverbs, chapter 4.

I always begin my sermons telling people to open their Bibles to the chapter I'm preaching on. I believe this does two things. First, it gets the chapter hunting and Bible page rustling out of the way right at the start, so we don't lose momentum once I've started. Second, my announcement signals that it is going to be a message not from my opinions but from the Bible itself.

Now I start the introduction. Note: I'll be discussing the introduction more fully in the next chapter.

As I was working my way through the Bible verses Mark chose for his baptism, I suddenly got to thinking of something I hadn't thought of for a long time: Green Stamps.

To some of you, the phrase "Green Stamps" means nothing, unless you think I'm talking about postage stamps that just happen to be green. But when I think of Green Stamps, I see a capital G and a capital S.

Because when I was Mark's age, growing up in the little town of Redfield, South Dakota, S&H Green Stamps were a major part of my American culture. Here's how they worked.

Mom would discover that she was running low on groceries, and she would send Dad into town with a list. Dad would drive over to a little mom-and-pop grocery store just east of the high school.

Dad would meander through the aisles, collecting canned corn and eggs and bread and butter and sugar, and would finally take everything to the checkout counter. Mr. Schevlin would ring up the purchases—in those days cash registers actually *rang.* And while Dad was getting out his cash or his checkbook, Mr. Schevlin was doing a bit of mental calculating. And after he'd given Dad his change, he would take out a sheet of green stamps and rip off a small section and give it to Dad. Dad would drop them into the brown paper grocery bag and drive home.

On the way home, of course, the Green Stamps would slither past the groceries to the bottom of the bag. And unless Mom was in too big a hurry as she unloaded all the groceries, she would spot the Green Stamps, take them out of the bag, and throw them into a drawer. And that would be the last anybody would think about them unless one of her kids happened to be hunting for something in that drawer.

Now, this cheerful neglect was exactly what the Green Stamp people were hoping would *not* happen. Because in that very same drawer was a blank booklet with a picture of some Green Stamps on the cover. What the Green Stamp people wanted my mom to do was to pause after her grocery unpacking, find that little booklet, and laboriously lick and stick Mr. Schevlin's stamps onto the pages.

And the Green Stamp people also wanted Mom to get out her S&H

Green Stamp catalog and look longingly through it at a new electric mixer or a new iron. They wanted Mom to see how many stamps were needed to buy those things, and they wanted Mom to count the stamps she'd already licked, discover that she didn't have enough, and go out and buy more things so that she could collect enough stamps and eventually get that mixer and that iron.

A lot of American mothers *did* follow through on this. These moms were faithful lickers-and-stickers, and a lot of their kids got bicycles that way. But my mom put stamp-sticking at a low priority. In fact, every once in a while Dad would be at the store and the checker would ask, "Need a new stamp book?" Dad would pause thoughtfully and say, "Maybe you'd better give me one just to make sure."

I'm going to skip over a couple of the sermon's paragraphs because of space limitations. In the part I'm omitting, I mention that Green Stamps are still being used, only now they're called Green Points, and are popular in some parts of the country. (In fact, if the store is on the Green Point program, the points are tallied electronically onto the cash register receipt.) Then I continue:

As I say, I was really startled to see that Green Stamps in their new format were still alive and well. But I guess it's no great surprise. There are a lot of other "point systems" out there—frequent flyer miles, and that little card you used to get at Subway that they stamped until you got a free sub, and many other bonus plans.

The point system is very much alive in schools, too. I'm guessing Mark's teacher has some kind of a point system for him and her other students. It's great for the classroom—it makes grading more fair and less subjective.

Here comes the transition.

However, not everything that works for the classroom works in a relationship with Jesus. Sure, Jesus is the Great Teacher, but He's not giving us grades based on points. That's because He wants to be *more* than a teacher—He wants to be our friend. When He comes back in the sky to take Mark to heaven, He's not going to count to see how many Green Stamps Mark has.

But what's chilling is that some people like a point system better than a relationship. In every generation there are Pharisees who would rather *not* come closer to God and get to know Him personally. Instead, they delight in making up regulations, rules, traditions, laws to obey, so that they can try to measure how many "points" God owes them because of what they have done for Him. That way, when they pray they can say proudly—like the Pharisee praying in the Temple—"*I* fast, *I* give tithes, *I* pray, *I* . . . *I* . . . *I* . . ."

But that attitude is so wrong.

And here's the approach sentence:

Jesus and the rest of the Bible tell us that the way to God is not points but a path—and the following verses from the chapter that Mark chose will tell you and me some ways to stay on that path.

"Ways" is the key word, and I'm promising my hearers I will reveal a few of those ways to them.

And now for the first SPICAT itself. The first thing I do is to start with the S—the scripture. I always read the verse or verses first, then state the point, not the other way around. Remember, I want to signal to my listeners that my points are going to be coming directly from the Bible. As I mentioned before, even though I have already inserted the Scripture passage into my manuscript, I read it aloud from the Bible I'm holding in my hand.

Proverbs 4:10: "Hear, my son, and receive my sayings, and the years of your life will be many."

The New King James Version is the Bible we have in our church pews, so that's the one I preach from, even though many in our congregation use the NIV. I always want to make sure that a newcomer will be able to grab a pew Bible and easily follow along. When one of my lay preacher evaluators read the previous sentence, he wrote, "Very important point! I often see people reaching for the pew Bibles, but if the version read from the pulpit is different, they end up closing the Bible. Not a good thing."

The next thing on the SPICAT list is the P, the statement of the point. And after a brief lead-in paragraph, that's exactly what I do. I make sure to emphasize the point on my sermon manuscript so that I won't treat it like any other sentence, but will emphasize it with my voice. Sometimes I'll make the signal even stronger: I'll say, "If you're taking sermon notes, here's point 1."

Back to the sermon:

Already we see something interesting in this Proverbs verse. Someone is talking, and he is talking to someone he considers a son. And this father figure urges this son to both "hear" and "receive" his sayings.

And both hearing and receiving are important. Because—

[point 1] I believe that the first way Mark and the rest of us can stay on Jesus' path is to listen actively.

And after the point comes a quick lead-in paragraph, and then the illustration.

[lead-in paragraph] In other words, "listen" to the Bible's wisdom, but also "receive" it. The NIV says "accept" this wisdom. Listen *actively*. *Receive* that wisdom.

[illustration] It's like playing in a football game. If you're one of the players who doesn't normally get to carry the ball much, you can just go along and have a general idea of where the ball is. But if somebody passes you the ball, you've got to wake up and *receive* it. You've got to take possession of that ball, and then you've got to go and *do* something with it.

And then follows the comment and the application.

[comment] Mark probably knows his Bible pretty well by now. Whenever he comes up against a temptation, the Holy Spirit might throw him a Bible text that warns about that temptation or shows what to do to avoid it.

[application] Rather than ignoring that Bible text, Mark needs to reach out and gather it in, and then run with it. And that's what we *all* need to do. Because the devil is out there with some pretty strong temptations. Remember what Jesus did when the devil tempted Him in the wilderness? He caught Bible verses from His memory, and then threw them at the devil. And the devil backed off. Scripture can give us this power too.

So that's a brief sample of part of a sermon. Remember, in future chapters we'll be dealing with the SPICAT elements in more detail. But for now, two more homework projects.

Homework Project 8—Buy a Stopwatch

Go to a sports store and buy a stopwatch. Smuggle it into church this weekend and time your pastor's sermon segments. If he or she isn't preaching an expository sermon, label the segments "Introduction," "Main Part," and "Conclusion/Appeal."

Homework Project 9—Discover Your Approach Sentence and Points

Prayerfully begin using your general notes to work toward an approach sentence and some points. *Note!* You will almost certainly not use *all* your general notes, because for the first several pages you were just feeling your way along. You'll feel sad for all those unusable pages, but don't try to force them into your current sermon. Even though your sermon may have changed direction, you will still have some thoughtful ideas there, so save them for future talks or devotionals you might give.

If You're Working on a Sermon Right Now

- *Keep praying!* "Help fine-tune these ideas, Lord! Own this sermon!"
- *By now you've probably decided* on the number of points your sermon will have. Working within a 30-minute sermon time line, allot a certain number of minutes to each of the following elements: introduction, transition, each SPICAT, and the conclusion/appeal.
- *Flip back through* the other "If You're Working on a Sermon Right Now" segments at the end of the previous chapters to make sure you haven't let anything slide.

GROUP DISCUSSION STARTERS

Nonjudgmental sharing time! Each group member should report on the sermon in progress, briefly describing the introduction, the transition/approach, and the SPICATs' points. *Vital:* No other group member should criticize or try to fine-tune unless help is specifically asked for. This is a *very fragile time* in the sermon-building process, and one unfeeling comment can shrivel enthusiasm—and a good sermon might evaporate.

Group members should divide into teams of two, Person A and Person B. Set a stopwatch or kitchen timer for five minutes. A and B should each take five minutes and try to communicate his or her sermon's essential message clearly to the other person, along with why he or she feels so passionate about it.

8

Chapter Outline:

The Sermon's Introduction

One afternoon while meeting with a group of Christian writers, I mentioned that I was writing this book. One of the writers perked up her ears.

"Tell your readers to do what your brother does," she suggested. (She's a member of the church that Chester pastors.)

"What's that?" I asked.

"Chester often starts his messages with a story," she said, "but he doesn't tell the end of it. He just leaves us hanging, and then he finishes it at the end of the sermon."

It is just one of several great ways to hold people's attention. But before we go any further, let me give you—by way of warning—an example of:

How *Not* to Introduce Your Sermon

"Good morning . . . Is this mike on? Can anybody hear me out there? Well, maybe I'll just speak louder and try to do without it. Oh, it *is* on? Are you sure? One-two-three. Testing-one-two-three. Ah, now I can hear it. Great. Oh, by the way, here are some announcements they wanted me to make right now because a lot of people weren't in the sanctuary at announcement time. *[The speaker then gives three announcements and has someone else come up to give a fourth. Then:]* Is it still raining outside? No? Great, great. We've really been having interesting weather this week, haven't we? I told my wife the other day that I don't think it's been this wet, this early, for years and years.

"But we certainly do need the rain, don't we? How many of you like rain? Let me see your hands. I see that some of you do and some of you don't, about half and half. What's wrong, Jim? I thought you *liked* rain! What's that? Oh, you don't like too *much* rain. Well, I guess that makes sense. How many of you *kids* like rain? Let me see your hands . . . Well, I hope all that moisture gets right down into the subsoil and stays there, so the crops'll really take hold next spring. Amen? *Amen!*"

Cozy, right? Chummy and friendly? Of course. But *not* a sermon intro. In fact, a large number of listeners—while striving to hold on to a friendly grin—are thinking, *If this guy likes moisture so much, why doesn't he go jump in the lake?* And they'll peek wistfully at their watches and wonder, *If it takes him this long to warm up, how long's it gonna take him to wind down?*

Another Way *Not* to Introduce Your Sermon

"In the third chapter of Joel, the prophet brings to our view a scene of the deepest and most meaningful significance. Scarcely ever in the annals of human history, with all its despair and eternal wanderings, has the heart of man been so shattered with discouragement; yet within the very adamantine core of the hardest heart, within the deepest inky blackness that surrounds the most benighted soul, an answering chord responds to the note of hope that Joel sounds, clear as a trumpet call . . ."

The blather in the paragraph above sounds like something that might have been written back in the mid-1800s, not to be spoken but to be read. And it's not good writing even by lush Victorian standards.

So let's come up with a better way, OK? How about *Jesus'* way?

Creating the Story Introduction

Grabbing and holding attention—with something that leads directly into the topic—is the first thing the sermon introduction should do. "In the introduction," a pastor friend of mine advises lay preachers, "tell me why I should listen to you."

Every once in a while the Gospels hint that even the Master Teacher Himself had to get people's attention:

"He taught them many things by parables, and in his teaching said: 'Listen! A farmer went out to sow his seed'" (Mark 4:2, 3, NIV).

"Listen!" must have been the first-century way of saying, "May I have your attention, please?" And once He got attention, what did Jesus do? *He immediately began telling a story.* No announcements, no rambling on about how "it's getting a bit cloudy out there over the Sea of Galilee, isn't it? I wonder if we'll have a storm." No flowery, padded, 1870s-era prose.

No, Jesus understood that telling a story is still the best way to grab attention and begin focusing it on God's Word. So don't waste time, don't make preliminary remarks—just get right into the story the way Jesus did. And as I mentioned a few paragraphs back, *make sure the story ties directly into the topic of the sermon, or at least the first SPICAT.*

Before we get to the nuts and bolts of all this, let me prove my point about how effective story introductions are. This morning while waiting in a doctor's office I glanced into the latest edition of *Reader's Digest.* I wrote down the first sentence or two of several articles. Notice how the author grabs your attention:

- *"A girl carrying groceries.* A stranger beckons her into his car."
- *"Soon after my father's death* by suicide, my mother and I stood in his closet, still sour-sweet with the smell of him, and stuffed his clothes into big black garbage bags."
- *"At 1:00 in the morning,* five days before Christmas last December, Jennifer Sneed was jolted awake by full-blown labor pains. Her due

date was still three weeks away, but the contractions were already coming two minutes apart."

- **"In an unadorned room** deep inside an Israeli maximum-security prison, a handsome Palestinian youth sits at a small wooden table across from television newscaster Barbara Walters. At age 17, the young man, who is now 21, attempted to set off a bomb on a crowded street to massacre as many people as possible, including himself."

Again, each of them was an introduction to an *article,* not a story. Yet in each case the author chose to use a dramatic story segment to catch and hold the readers' attention.

Where do you get your introduction's story? From the illustration file you've been building as you've been reading this book. For example—

- *Use stories from your childhood.* As I mentioned back in chapter 3, relate stories about yourself, but don't make yourself the hero. And if possible, tell the story until you get to the cliff-hanger part—the most exciting spot, where your hearers are dying to find out what happens next—and then segue into your sermon, saving the finish until the sermon's end. You can of course do this with any kind of story, childhood or not.

An important rule of thumb about childhood or any other reality-based stories is to always change the names of the people (unless you're telling a nonlibelous story about a well-known public figure), and explain to the congregation what you're doing, even when the story's events aren't negative but positive. More and more churches are putting MP3 audio sermon files on the Web, and somebody back in your old hometown might get an unpleasant surprise while surfing the Internet some evening to find himself or herself the villain of a story that literally can go around the world in a few seconds. *Remember,* even if a story's events are positive and even heroic, it still distresses many people to find themselves spotlighted in this way.

- *Use stories from current events.* If you employ contemporary news stories, try to go deeper and get information the average person isn't likely to discover on TV or radio broadcasts. Search online newspapers, local or national.

And like a good reporter, make sure you verify a fact from one or two other sources before you use it. Right now Shelley and I are reading *Reporting Live,* CBS journalist Lesley Stahl's superb autobiography of her career, which began during the Watergate era. She mentions again and again that her bosses at the network always insisted that reporters couldn't report rumor—a story always had to be verified before it was put on the air.

This is old news to you if you're familiar with the Internet at all. You simply can't believe everything you read there. Even breaking news from CNN or the other reputable networks can change from hour to hour as more facts become available.

- **Use stories from history.** Shakespeare knew this very well. When he wrote such plays as Hamlet or Macbeth, he didn't make it all up out of his own head. Instead, he based their plots on historical events the people already knew something about. Many pastors read biographies and autobiographies, and this gives their sermons depth and significance— and also inspires congregation members to do more worthwhile reading themselves.

Other Kinds of Introductions

"Wait a minute," someone might protest at this point. "Do I always have to start my sermon by an attention-grabber? Isn't this just pandering to people's desire to be entertained?"

Well, if that's the case, we could bring the same charge against Jesus Himself, because Mark 4:34 states that He didn't even speak to the people unless He told a parable. The Bible is full of God's creative attempts to get our attention, everything from the gold and purple wilderness sanctuary (which illustrated how sin was dealt with) to prophets who described the future with visions featuring fantastic beasts and dragons. And the Bible itself, end to end, is awash with stories.

While I'm frankly sold on the story intro, other kinds of introductions do exist, such as:

- **The question introduction.** "Have you ever awakened at 2:30 a.m. and lain there wondering, 'Am I really saved? If I were to suffer an instant brain aneurysm right now, with no time to think about my salvation, what would happen to me?'"

It is such a gripping introduction that you probably won't have to arouse your listeners' interest any more than this. So you'd immediately use a transition statement, such as: "Fortunately, God inspired [Bible writer] to calm our fears on this very point. Please take your Bibles and open them to [Bible chapter]." And then you'd go right into your first SPICAT.

- **The quote introduction.** "C. S. Lewis' book *The Screwtape Letters* is a series of letters written by a devil named Screwtape to his nephew Wormwood. The letters are filled with the older devil's advice on how to corrupt humanity and cause them to be lost. At one point Screwtape says, 'The safest road to Hell is the gradual one—the gentle slope, soft underfoot, without sudden turnings, without milestones, without signposts.' That's chilling, isn't it? But it's true. In fact, that's very close to what Jesus Himself says in Matthew 7:13."

And then you'd go right into a good approach sentence (such as: "Fortunately, in [Bible chapter] Jesus gives us four important principles that will keep us off that gentle slope and turn us toward heaven instead"). Then launch into your first SPICAT.

- *The parable introduction.* (Once in a while you might write an introduction in parable form. This example employs a real event I saw while driving one day. If I were to use it as a parable introduction, I'd write it like this:) "The kingdom of heaven is like unto a woman I saw the other day. She was pushing her tiny baby in a stroller along the sidewalk past the Walgreen drugstore about eight blocks north of here. If you've seen that corner, you know that the landscapers raised the drugstore's parking lot about five or six feet above the sidewalk level, but they put in a cement staircase."

I would then go on to tell how the woman tipped the stroller so that one front wheel was on the first step, then tipped it the other way to place the other wheel on the second step. She repeated this again and again until she was at the top. During this climb the baby flopped from side to side in the stroller, sometimes nearly tipping out, but didn't seem worried. Even though the child's whole world was rocking, and even though the mother's face couldn't be seen, the baby trusted her. That is the attitude we need to take toward our invisible heavenly Parent.

More About Transitions

Here's another golden sermon rule: *If you know how to create good transitions, your congregation can't help listening to your sermon.*

Transitions can be large (sentences or even paragraphs, as I've already shown). Or they can be single words, as I'll mention below. However long or short they are, they're bridges that you build for your hearers so they can easily move from one idea to another.

The good news is that you're already using transitions very naturally in your conversation. So it's just a matter of understanding how to let them flow into your sermon.

Here are some lists of transitional words:

- *Transitional tags:* words such as *and, but, for, however, moreover, nevertheless, nor, on the other hand, or, so, yet.*
- *Addition transitions: again, also, and, and then, besides, equally important, finally, first, further, furthermore, in addition, in the first place, last, moreover, next, second, still, too.*
- *Comparison transitions: also, in the same way, likewise, similarly.*
- *Concession transitions: granted, naturally, of course.*
- *Contrast transitions: although, and yet, at the same time, but at the same time, despite that, even so, even though, for all that, however, in contrast, in spite of, instead, nevertheless, notwithstanding, on the contrary, on the other hand, otherwise, regardless, still, though, yet.*
- *Emphasis transitions: certainly, indeed, in fact, of course.*
- *Example transitions: after all, as an illustration, even, for example, for instance, in conclusion, indeed, in fact, in other words, in short, it is true, namely, of course, specifically, that is, thus, to illustrate, truly.*
- *Summary transitions: all in all, altogether, as has been said, finally, in brief, in conclusion, in other words, in particular, in short, in simpler terms, in summary, on the whole, that is, therefore, to put it differently, to summarize.*
- *Time sequence transitions: after a while, afterward, again, also, and then, as long as, at last, at length, at that time, before, besides, earlier, eventually, finally, formerly, further, furthermore, in addition, in the first place, in the past, last, lately, meanwhile, moreover, next, now, presently, second, shortly, simultaneously, since, so far, soon, still, subsequently, then, thereafter, too, until, until now, when.*

Here's just one example of how to use several of these words and phrases.

> I spent most of my boyhood on a tiny farm in South Dakota. **And** since the Dakotas are pretty much halfway between the highly cultured coasts of this country, I sometimes felt as though history was passing me by. **However,** the more I thought about my pioneer immigrant ancestors, the more I realized that it took a strong brand of courage to leave a homeland and a language behind, and journey to what turned out to be a barren, treeless landscape.
>
> **In the same way,** it took real courage to cling to their land while the Great Depression dust storms howled over their cabins. **Of course,** most Dakota homesteaders didn't

have a lot of extra cash to pay moving expenses. **Still,** those who scraped the dust out of their teeth and hoped for a rainy spring had learned a lot about life's deadly realities.

Therefore, I come from a heritage of fortitude—*even though* some might call it "stubbornness." **And** I've done my best to keep a balance. **On the one hand,** I hope I've learned to treasure that stubbornness, **yet** I've struggled to modify it with an eye open to other points of view.

Homework Project 10—Notice Transitions in Everyday Life

Starting now, and for the next 24 hours, keep your eyes open for transitions—in commercials, news stories, reading, and conversation. Write them down if you're where you can do that. Study how the most effective ones keep you alert and interested in the message being communicated.

If You're Working on a Sermon Right Now

- *Keep praying!* "Lord, help me hold on to my hearers' attention!"
- *Definitely decide on your sermon's introduction and transition.* Like Jesus, you should avoid preliminary chitchat and get right into the story. *Remember* to follow your allotted time (ideally, not more than 10-15 percent of the entire sermon time for introduction and transition combined).
- *Go back to the lists of transitional words and phrases* in this chapter and read them all *aloud.* That will help fix them in your mind.

GROUP DISCUSSION STARTERS

If you have time, brave group members can stand to their feet and actually give their sermon introduction as they plan to preach it. Ask someone to time it. For a 30-minute sermon, the introduction should be no longer than three to five minutes.

This group session would be a great time to swap illustrations or brainstorm about things that happened during the day that could become illustrations.

Often I've found it helpful to rewrite my SPICAT outline, and maybe group members could have a few minutes to do this. It's surprising how going through the outline again will often clarify points, comments, and applications.

9

Chapter Outline:

The Layman Who Read Isaiah

One day when I was in my 20s I sat in a worship service in a tiny church and watched as a layman stepped up to the pulpit. This man, I knew, hadn't had the chance to get a lot of education, and had grown up speaking a language other than English. So I wondered how his sermon would go.

He asked us to open our Bibles to Isaiah. I don't remember which chapter he chose—probably one of the messianic ones, such as 53 or 61. We obediently flipped to the passage and settled down to wait.

And then he simply started to read.

His reading was not quick and glib, but slow and careful. The Bible was a sacred book to him, and he did not wish to stumble over its words. So he read slowly and humbly, feeling his way along, word by word.

And as he read, tears filled his voice. As each phrase came from his lips, I almost felt as though the prophet Isaiah were speaking to us, in warm tones of concern. I found tears welling up in my own eyes.

Eventually he finished the chapter and began to talk about it. While I have forgotten what he said from that point on, I do remember how he brought us reverently near to Isaiah's own agony as the prophet interceded for a rebellious nation. I felt very close to God during that worship service.

That day I discovered how important it is to read the Bible aloud in an effective way. That's what I'd like to talk about next. But first let's find out—

How *Not* to Read the Bible Aloud

The man I described above was a delightful exception when it came to Bible readers. However, many lay preachers fall into one of several camps:

- *The bumblers.* Bumblers haven't practiced reading their verses aloud. So when they're behind the pulpit, they make false starts. They stumble over Bible names. If a sentence takes up two verses, they'll stop at the end of the first verse—even though it's not the end of the Bible writer's sentence—and they'll pause in confusion, vaguely sensing that something is wrong. Finally they'll lurch ahead, not realizing that they've just derailed the train of thought.
- *The insurance-clause reciters.* These people read Scripture in a low, foggy monotone, as though they're reciting the fine print in an insurance contract or reading a report into the *Congressional Record.* Maybe they think "monotone" equals "reverent." Perhaps they suspect it's sacrilegious to read the Bible expressively. But at the same time they're sending a chilling signal to the children in the congregation:

> *Yes, Jesus bores me,*
> *Yes, Jesus bores me,*
> *Yes, Jesus bores me,*
> *The Bible bores me too.*

- *The M-16 rifle full-auto mode.* Such speakers take a breath and rattle through Scripture's immortal prose as if they're mowing down pop-up targets during week 6 of Army basic training, using the older M-16s on which you could flip the selector to "full automatic" and empty a 20-round clip in a couple seconds. Christ's heart-cries to the Pharisees; His

103

gentle encouragement to the woman caught in adultery; His agonies on the cross—all get flung out as carelessly as a string of "begats."

• *The whiners/beseechers.* These individuals have decided that Bible passages should be delivered in a droopy sing-song, like someone trying to call a cat down from a tree. The signal sent: "Reading the Bible requires a 'special' voice tone. Therefore it's probably much too 'special' for an average sinner like me."

• *The impersonators.* Fortunately, I think this breed is rare. But every once in a while you come across someone who tries to read the Bible (or preach) like Billy Graham, T. D. Jakes, Rick Warren, Luis Palau, Max Lucado, Bill Hybels, or some other well-known pastor. Impersonators need to drop the pose and get real.

Here, for your consideration, are some suggestions about—

How *to* Read the Bible Aloud

• *Read naturally.* When you read the Bible aloud, *your goal should be to disappear.* Don't try to do so through a mousy monotone—instead, disappear by being your ordinary self. Because any attempt to read verses in a manner that isn't "you" calls attention to itself and makes people wonder why you're treating God's Word that way.

• *Read clearly.* Some people read as though they're in the last stages of lockjaw, or they're ventriloquists trying not to move their lips. Others let their jaws go slack, and barely click their consonants at all. Tape-record yourself reading the Bible, and let someone else listen to it. Turn the volume lower and lower. Even though your voice is getting fainter, the listener should still be able to understand your words. If you're not saying your consonants clearly, start practicing. Listen carefully to TV or radio newscasters and study how they speak clearly while sounding natural.

• *Read interpretively*—as though you're reading an adventure story aloud to a group of 9-year-olds. I don't mean ham it up, but vary your voice rate and tone. Kids (who are the most honest among us) will doze off at the drone of an insurance-clause reciter. They'll grow restless and hostile at the full-auto rattle of an M-16. And they'll snicker at the whiner/beseecher or giggle at the impersonator.

So you've got to give them something authentic—but interesting. Take this passage, for example:

"Nevertheless the people refused to obey the voice of Samuel; and they said, 'No, but we will have a king over us, that we also may be like all the nations, and that our king may judge us and go out before us and fight our battles'" (1 Sam. 8:19, 20).

Let me show you a very effective technique to guide you toward doing some great interpretive reading. The first thing to do is to break up the lines into bite-size segments, into units of thought, sort of like lines of poetry.

> "Nevertheless,
>> the people refused to obey the voice of Samuel;
>> and they said,
>> 'No, but we will have a king over us,
>> that we also may be like all the nations,
>> and that our king may
>>> judge us
>>> and go out before us
>>> and fight our battles.'"

That's merely one of several ways to handle the passage—you can divide it differently if you like. The main thing is to break the passage down into little units of thought. I'd suggest that you type or print out your Bible verse(s) that way, and practice reading, *pausing slightly at the end of each line.* Just that tip alone should enhance your listeners' appreciation by about 25 percent.

But you can do even more. Here's the passage again. This time, put more emphasis on the **bolded, *italicized*** words. *Don't* say them more loudly than the others, but instead, *allow the pitch of your voice to rise slightly.* Put more expression into those words and phrases. Pause a bit where the dots are. Try it.

> "***Nevertheless,*** . . .
>> the people refused to **obey** the voice of Samuel; . . .
>> and they said, . . .
>> 'No, but we ***will*** have a king ***over*** us, . . .
>> that ***we*** . . . ***also*** . . . may be **like** all the ***nations,*** . . .
>> and that our king may
>>> ***judge*** us . . .
>>> and ***go out before us*** . . .
>>> and ***fight our battles.'"***

You get the idea, right? (And by the way, the words I've emphasized aren't the only "right" ones. There are other ways to read that passage expressively, depending on the point you're trying to make.) As long as you don't make your reading seem too artificial, your listeners will deeply appreciate this effort to bring the Bible to life. And the kids might listen as carefully to you as I listened to the humble layman read Isaiah!

- **Rehearse.** As you rehearse your sermon, *practice reading the Bible passages, too.* I never skip this part, because what the *Bible* actually says is vastly more important than what my sermon does.

- **Mark your Bible for reading.** I have a Bible that I use only for preaching. It's a thinline New King James Version (the same version as our sanctuary's pew Bibles), and it's light enough to hold in my left hand without weighing me down. When I need to use both hands, I lay the Bible on the edge of the pulpit in the sight of the people. I'll never forget what someone said to me more than 15 years ago, just after I arrived at the church I currently pastor: "I really appreciate how you make the Bible so visible when you preach."

Since I give expository sermons, I'm dealing with a longish passage that I will deliver to the congregation a few verses at a time. To avoid glancing away from my Bible to the manuscript to remind myself of what verse to end on, I use a soft, easily erasable pencil to draw short slanted lines on the Bible page, at the beginning and end of each segment I want to read. That way I can focus completely on the passage, and concentrate on reading it well. When I get to the end mark, I stop and return to the manuscript.

Transitions Between Sermon Points

Glance back at the transitions section in the previous chapter, because you'll be using the same approach here. The only difference is that in the last chapter we talked about transitioning from your introduction to your sermon itself, and here we're talking about transitioning between the SPICATs.

In a minute I'm going to give you an example of an effective transition between two sermon points, but first take a look at—

A Couple of *Bad, Bad* Transitions Between Sermon Points
- *"OK. So much for point 1.* Now here's point 2."

Why is that such a bad transition? Because it smacks of a supermarket shopping list—we've bought the dishwashing detergent, so now it's time to hurry over to the next aisle and get the baking powder. Also, that transition doesn't do one single thing to get us *interested* in point 2.

- *"**Whoa. Look at the time.** It's noon already. I've got two more points I need to cover, but I'll be as quick as I can. Bear with me—here comes point 2."*

No comment needed, right?

When a pastor friend read the "no comment needed" line immediately above, he told me, "Go ahead and comment anyway. It needs to be stressed."

So here's my observation. Just how effective do you really think those "two more points" are going to be after a transition like that? For one thing, the speaker mentioned the time, which is a no-no. For another thing, the speaker didn't keep the listeners *encouraged* and *enthused*. "You ain't heard *nothin'* yet," your SPICAT transitions should say. "The best is yet to come!"

An Example of a Better Transition Between Sermon Points

A couple months ago I preached a sermon on John 21. The approach sentence was something like "In John 21 Jesus gives us four reasons to become or remain His disciples." My points were:

- *Point 1: Jesus satisfies my hunger for God's Word.*
- *Point 2: Jesus proves that when He wants to, He can take total control of the details of my everyday life.*
- *Point 3: Jesus will bring me to the point where I understand my own sinfulness.*
- *Point 4: Jesus calls me to His service.*

To give you a flavor of how a transition between sermon points works, let me print out a few paragraphs of the sermon. I've just stated point 2, and at the end of the paragraphs below I transition to point 3. I've **bolded and italicized** the transition sentence.

> You see, Jesus is never far from the gritty realities of life. He's been in carpentry and construction since His childish fingers could hold a nail. He knows very well what it takes to earn a living and to build up a good business reputation. He knows how hard times can dry up the cash flow really fast.
>
> But He also knows that His heavenly Father watches

over each workplace, each neighborhood, each home, with a fatherly gaze. He knows that with God's kindly eye on His children, we don't need to worry. Hard work is good, and creative marketing is good, and success techniques are good. Proverbs has a lot to say about intelligent, methodical labor, not only by men but by women, as Proverbs 31 shows.

But every worker, every artist, every teacher, every manager or supervisor or business owner, needs to say, at the end of every day, "Thank You, Lord, for making this possible."

And every person who's had a bad week at the job, or who has no job to have a bad week *at,* or who is going through any other kind of discouragement, needs to say, "I trust You, Lord. Help me tomorrow. Give me patience, and give me wisdom to position myself for the good things You have in store for me."

TRANSITION TO NEXT POINT: But Jesus is much more than a solver of business crises.

At this point the sermon moves naturally into point 3, which is *"Jesus will bring me to the point where I understand my own sinfulness."* In the transition sentence I tried to do two things: (1) tie the previous point to the upcoming one, and (2) show that Jesus has still more important things to share with us than what we've seen thus far in the sermon.

You can have a lot of latitude in transition statements. I find that if my Bible chapter contains a story, and I'm working my way through that story as I bring out my sermon points, I don't feel as much need for enticing transitions, because the story itself will keep the people interested, and because it provides the bridges that help people follow you from idea to idea.

The Conclusion/Appeal

It's extremely important to provide some kind of conclusion or appeal at the end of your message. A sermon without some kind of opportunity for response often ends up as little more than a lecture.

"Good point!" says an experienced African-American lay preacher who read my manuscript. "In Black churches the 'call' typically gives people an opportunity to declare their choice for Jesus, and is given with each sermon. Worship is not considered complete unless the 'door of fellowship' is opened to all who will come."

Your local congregation's culture will give you some guidelines here. Some churches are used to hearing a come-forward call nearly every week, while others are more accustomed to responding inwardly. You might want to ask your pastor for guidance on this, and listen carefully to how he or she concludes a sermon.

Here are elements I normally include in my own conclusions/appeals:

- *A restatement of the sermon points, or at least a reference to the main theme.* I do this as quickly and creatively as I can. I don't simply read off the points—I generally combine them into a sentence.
- *A call for response.* Most of the time I have people raise their hands, but sometimes I ask them to stand. Make sure the appeal is a specific one, so that they'll know for sure what they're responding to.

Here are a few sermon conclusions I've given recently:

From the John 21 sermon above:

> *I don't know where you are, spiritually, this morning. But I do know that every once in a while I need to follow Simon Peter's path again. [Note to reader: here comes a recap of the sermon points.] I need to learn a hunger for Scripture, I need to trust Jesus with my day, I need to discover again how sinful I am, and then say yes when Jesus calls me to follow Him and serve Him. And right now I'm going to say yes to Jesus again. I'm going to ask Him to guide me through the week ahead. Would you like to say yes to Him too?*

From a Thanksgiving Day sermon titled "Thanksgiving at Jesus' House." (Note: In this conclusion I *don't* recap the sermon points.)

> *One of the most heartbreakingly beautiful things you and I need to thank Jesus for is that, for all my talk about going to Jesus' house for Thanksgiving, He never really had a literal house. In Luke 9:58 Jesus said that even the little animals such as foxes had their own dens, but He Himself didn't have anywhere to lay His head. Jesus had no earthly mansion as the headquarters of His heavenly mission.*

> *And even when He told us about heaven in John 14, He*

didn't say, "In my house are many mansions." He said, "In my Father's house are many mansions."

But Jesus isn't homeless. He does have a dwelling place here on earth. In Matthew 18:20 He tells us where He lives: "For where two or three are gathered together in My name, I am there in the midst of them." Paul tells us in Colossians 1:27 that Christ can be in us, and that this can be the hope of a future glory.

So this room, right here, is Jesus' house today. We are indeed having Thanksgiving at Jesus' house. When you sit around the tables at our banquet once this service is over, each of those tables is Jesus' house.

How about it? Would you like to make Him feel welcome today? Let's talk to Him about it right now. [I conclude with prayer.]

From a sermon called "Why We Need Him," which I will discuss in the next chapter.

If you died apart from God, God would grieve. And He would grieve not with puny human grief, but with great, sobbing, heavenly cries. "How can I give you up?" He would sob. "How can I let you go?"

Let's not put Him through that, OK? Let's recognize how much we need Him, and His Son, and His Holy Spirit. Let's assure Him [here's where I recap the sermon points] *that we know He's truthful, self-sacrificing, and desperately relevant to our day-to-day lives. And let's cling so closely to Him that when He appears in the sky above us, we can take our first electric, immortal breath and shout a greeting to our King of Glory.* [We then sang "Hail Him the King of Glory" as a response song.]

Homework Project 11—Notice Transitions in Sermons You Hear

Here is another "find the transitions" exercise. But this time, as you listen to a sermon by your pastor—or a radio or TV preacher—write down the ways he or she glides from sermon point to sermon point.

If You're Working on a Sermon Right Now
* *Keep praying!* "Lord, give me courage and humility!"

- *Fill in the SPICAT content needed* for each of your sermon points. Keep to your time frames! And don't forget that your hearers are going to have only one chance to hear (not read) your message. Make it cheerful and user-friendly.
- *Begin to rehearse parts of your sermon* (or the entire sermon if you've pretty much completed it). Constantly revise for ease of understanding (theirs and yours)!
- *Remember to write (and speak) naturally!* There's a difference between an article written for print and a sermon composed for the ear.
- *As you rehearse, pay close attention to how you read* your Bible passages aloud. Hand your Bible to a spouse or a friend. Ask them to read the verses aloud to you, and listen carefully. If you hear them do it effectively, incorporate that technique into your own presentation.
- *Mark your Bible chapter with a soft pencil* so that you can clearly see when to begin and end each segment you read.
- *Pay special attention to the T parts* of the SPICATs.

GROUP DISCUSSION STARTERS

Think back to the sermons you've heard preached by laypersons. Which sermons—or which lay speakers—have stayed in your mind? Why? What affected you more—the logical content or the emotional content? Was there something in the layperson's preaching style you found effective (use of voice, gestures, etc.)? What did you consider ineffective? Tell the rest of the group about this.

Divide into teams of two. Each team member should read his or her preaching passage aloud, expressively, to the other, and the other should respond with a "3-1 critique" (three positive comments and one suggestion for improvement).

Find out which group member's preaching passage is the shortest, and have that person go to the board and rewrite all or part of the passage into "poetry lines," as instructed in this chapter. The group should then offer suggestions about which words or phrases should be emphasized. (Note: there are many possible ways to read a passage aloud.)

The group leader should interview a volunteer about an exciting or emotional or dramatic thing that's happened to him or her, or why he or she loves a certain hobby, or anything else that is very easy and fun to talk about. Other group members should have paper and pencil at the ready, and should take down as many of the transitional words or phrases as the volunteer uses.

Each group member should talk about the conclusion/appeal he or she plans for the sermon.

10

Chapter Outline:

The Big Day—Some Suggestions

One morning many years ago, when I was a solemn young pastor not yet ordained, I arrived at my North Seattle church to discover that the ministerial director of my conference had set up a video camera about eight pews away from me. He cheerfully reassured me that it was part of my training and that one day he and I would sit down together, watch the video, and evaluate my preaching.

As it happens, I was ordained shortly afterward, and he and I never had our little evaluation session, which secretly relieved me. (The ministerial director was a great guy, but it filled me with horror to think about sitting down and watching myself preach!) Years later, when he was cleaning out his office, he handed me the video with an apologetic chuckle.

My wife and I watched it in the privacy of our family room—and did more than chuckle! Especially when we pushed the fast forward button! It was immediately and painfully clear that I had two distinctive preaching mannerisms. One was to adjust my glasses about every four or five sentences. I don't think plastic lenses had become common yet, and my heavy glass eyepieces would slide slowly down the bridge of my nose. Absentmindedly I would shove them up again and carry on, completely unaware of what was happening.

My other mannerism was what I did with my hands when I wasn't adjusting my glasses. I would be preaching along, making my points, telling my stories, and getting my ideas across. And while I was doing this, my hands were in the air, about chest height, a foot or so apart in karate-chop positions. Sometimes it seemed (especially on fast forward) as though I was actually *doing* karate chops, or maybe trying to play rapid Guatemalan marimba tunes with my little fingers. At other moments it appeared as though I were sliding large, invisible boxes of laundry detergent along pantry shelves.

More recently I've discovered another mannerism. I gulp. I first noticed the habit when I started listening to my sermons on tape to make sure I was speaking slowly and understandably. It seems that after I say something I hope will be humorous, I swallow nervously. This causes a little *glurp* that comes across clearly on the tape, probably because I use a lapel mike and slide it fairly far up my necktie to help give me what I hope is a warm, conversational tone. Fortunately neither my wife nor anybody else I've asked seems to have heard this over the sound system, and I've been working on silencing it for those who listen by tape.

Should your own preaching date be coming up soon, here are some final suggestions. If I could boil them down into one sentence, it would be this:

As a lay preacher, you should try to create the smallest amount of distraction possible between your hearers and the message God has given you for them.

Here are some ways to do this:

Dress Discreetly

Men, dress at least as formally as your pastor does. If he wears a suit and tie, you should too. Should you dress more casually, there's a strong chance that some people will miss the point of your message because they'll be getting a sour stomach from what they see as your lack of reverence in God's house.

Women, dress the way a female pastor would. The facts of life are that if your outfit accentuates your curves, or your neckline dips to a certain level, men who do not wish to sin with their eyes will not look at you, and you will become nothing more than a radio broadcast. And men who *don't* mind sinning with their eyes will largely ignore your sermon.

A Nuts-and-Bolts Guide to Preparing Your Sermon Notes

- *Use one side of the paper only.* Let me give you a couple reasons. First, you won't need to turn the sheets over, an action that's often visible from the pews and that might prompt whispered teenage betting about how many pages your sermon contains. Also, using one side of the paper will lessen the chance that you'll lose your place. *Where's the side I want? Where am I?*
- *Make sure the print is readable when you're standing up.* As you work on your outline, you're sitting down, and the print is close to your eyes. But when you're standing behind the pulpit, print that's too small might cause you to dip your head and even slump. For my sermon manuscripts I use Microsoft Word's 13-point Courier font, double-spaced, with fairly wide margins.
- *Double-space.* As one of my manuscript evaluators says, "I double-space so that I can write in any last-minute thoughts, or correct mistakes, without having my corrections 'leak over' onto other lines."
- *Revise (almost) to the very end.* Every morning that I preach I'm up at 5:00 a.m. reading my manuscript out loud, a black-ink fountain pen or felt pen in my hand. I underline words I want to emphasize or cross out whole sentences that I discover that I don't need. In the margins I carefully print other sentences that I have discovered that I *do* need. If something sounds too formal, I'll rework it so that it sounds natural and conversational. But I do not continue reading or revising as I'm sitting on the platform waiting to speak!
- *Bend up the corners of your notes.* This way you can easily get hold of a sheet when you're done with it, and slide it sideways across the pulpit.
- *Fold the sheets print side out so they fit within your Bible cover.* Your hearers might go into shock if they see you bringing a three-ring notebook or even a legal pad portfolio into the pulpit. *Oh, boy, this is gonna be a long one,* they'll think. Inside my own Bible cover every week I conceal a 27-page manuscript that would give heart failure to people who didn't know that I'm always a 30-minutes-and-under

speaker! (Why fold the sheets print side out? So they'll stay open on the pulpit.)

Using the Bible in the Pulpit

- *Invest in a "preaching Bible."* What's a preaching Bible? It's one you use only when giving sermons, and should be light enough to hold easily in one hand. Mine has no underlining (except the soft-pencil slashes that tell me where to start and stop reading during my sermon), no study notes, no massive concordance in the back. I don't store anything in this Bible (except the rubber bands I mention in the next paragraph)—no old church bulletins or clippings or fancy ribbons or tithe envelopes. Murphy's Law will make sure that these will flutter out of your Bible at precisely the moment you're hoping that your hearers are concentrating on a vital word from the Lord.
- *Use rubber bands to mark texts.* I think that every congregation has a subconscious anxiety about a speaker who has difficulty finding his or her Bible passages while in the pulpit.

But this is easily solved. If your Bible has an attached marker ribbon, that should be positioned to mark your preaching chapter, so that you can turn to it instantly as your sermon begins. Should you also want your hearers to turn to other verses, mark those pages by tucking tiny rubber bands into the binding where the pages come together, at the top of your Bible. During the sermon you can easily spot the crack where the rubber bands are, and go right to the text. (Thank you, evangelist Jack Bohannan, for that hint!)

- *Another option for marking passages.* A layperson who preaches a lot gives this suggestion: "I use the removable multicolor Post-it slim tabs. They won't leave marks in my Bible, and I can coordinate the color tabs to my manuscript."
- *Hold your Bible in your hand as you read it.* Let your hearers see where your truths are coming from. This is one time that I break the "look at your hearers" rule (which I talk about below). When I'm reading my Bible passage aloud, I keep my eyes on the page. I don't want people to think I'm ad-libbing. And by the way, don't make a habit of inserting your own explanatory comments as you read. Instead, use voice variation to get the meaning across.

Taming the Microphone

- *Know thy audiovisual person.* If your church has a good sound system and alert audiovisual people who've shown a track record of knowing what they're doing, you won't have to worry as much. But every once in a while you'll come up against an AV person who's a daydreamer or who thinks that once he or she has adjusted the volume to one individual's voice, that same volume will work just as well for everybody else—even if they're shorter, taller, louder, or softer. Some AV people also assume that if they're hearing you fine back at the AV booth—or through the earphones clamped to their head—everybody else in the sanctuary is hearing you perfectly too. But experienced AV people know that every sanctuary has dead spots, and they try to adjust for them.

- *Check the mike out ahead of time.* Do this *not* at the start of the sermon but earlier, when there are few—or no—people in the room. Listen to what you sound like over the speakers. A good rule of thumb: If you can hear yourself comfortably over the sound system, your audience will probably also.

- *Don't hesitate to get the sound adjusted if necessary.* If you're preaching along and you suddenly don't hear yourself anymore, glance back at the audiovisual people while you continue to talk. If they're bending anxiously over the sound board, obviously trying to fix something, give them a few more seconds to see if they can get the system to work. But if they're daydreaming, or chatting with each other, they may not know anything's wrong.

  If this happens, I tap the mike a couple times. Should I not hear any answering *thump-thump,* I'll pause in my sermon and tactfully say, "You know, I don't believe I'm getting much sound out of this." *Do not be shy about consulting the audiovisual people during the sermon.* Remember, your first responsibility is to the congregation.

- *Use the microphone correctly.* I prefer a lapel mike, worn high on my necktie, just under the knot. As I mentioned a few paragraphs back, this means that the mike also picks up any faint glurps I make (and I'm working to control these), but I want that mike high so that I don't have to raise my voice like an old-fashioned orator or risk a feedback squeal. In recent years microphone manufacturers have come up with a newer kind of mike that hooks over your ear and has a thin plastic tube that comes around the side of your cheek like a headset. It works wonderfully.

Never assume that a pulpit mike will make you sound good no matter what position it's in. And by all means, don't be shy of it. I know people who don't like to hear themselves over a sound system, so they will actually step away from the mike, thus making themselves inaudible to everyone except those in the first row. (And since nobody sits in the first row, nobody hears them!) Should you give in to mike fright and back away, it will force your vigilant AV person to slowly turn up the volume, and soon a high, ringing whistle will accompany your thoughtful remarks.

So get hold of that mike right at the start, and adjust it so that you're speaking directly into it. Don't get any closer than about eight or nine inches, however, or your *p's* and *b's* will sound like the local National Guard unit holding artillery practice in the baptistry.

Delivering Your Sermon

- *Avoid dead air.* Dead air is what you hear on a radio station when something goes wrong with the transmitter or the programming. It's a ghastly silence that may last only eight to 10 seconds but seems like a minute or two.

  Dead air is also what happens in a sanctuary during too much silence or inactivity, and it can give people the illusion that time is passing with yawning slowness. My church's worship services always have a vocal or instrumental musical selection just before my sermon. Once the performer has stepped away from the pulpit, I immediately take his or her place. After saying a sentence or two of thanks to give the singer a chance to sit down, I immediately begin my introduction.

  Dead air can happen in a sermon, too, and it's mainly because the speaker has lost his or her place (or train of thought!) and is trying to find it again. That is why rehearsal is so important. Just remember that even small bits of dead air cause discouragement and impatience in a congregation. *However, pauses for effect are OK—and necessary.* I mark them in my manuscript with a couple diagonal ink slashes.

- *Don't apologize or put yourself down.* Just launch into your introduction. People are nervous enough for you as it is. Just look them in the eye and get going, and that will put them at ease. They want you to succeed, and they will squirm with pity and discomfort if you dwell on how unfit you are to occupy the pulpit. *Remember: a sincere layperson is not an "intruder" in the pulpit. Nearly all the Bible prophets and preachers came from the laity.*

- *Stand in one place.* Don't wander aimlessly. Drifting about the platform may make you feel loose and tremendously at ease, but unless you're a trained actor—or unless each little journey across the platform has a purpose and has been carefully rehearsed—you will inspire restlessness among your hearers, and they'll lose most of your train of thought. I learned this back in college when I took an acting class. The instructor told us that movement always takes attention away from words. So unless your motions match your message, don't make them. Remember, your goal is to do nothing that distracts your hearers from the Bible message.

  Culture can affect this, of course. "In Black churches," an African-American lay preacher commented, "speakers have a tendency to 'break away' from the pulpit from time to time." But this layperson agrees that there shouldn't be wandering or drifting.

- *Look at your hearers.* I don't mean your eye has to move systematically down each row, locking eyes with each worshipper in turn. And I *certainly* don't suggest that you should lock eyes with one individual and hold him or her in a 30-second hypnotic stare. Just let your eyes move casually from area to area. If you don't feel comfortable looking into individual eyes, just keep your gaze where the people are. Don't bury your chin in your chest and stare at your notes or at the floor. Also don't gaze dreamily up at the ceiling or out the window. As I mentioned several paragraphs back, the only time I break the "look at your hearers" rule is when I'm reading aloud from the Bible. But while I'm doing that, I'm holding the Bible in one hand so that it's almost at eye level with my hearers.

After the Sermon

- *Accept thanks—and criticism—gracefully.* After the service, as you're standing at the door greeting the congregation, the overwhelming majority of those who comment on your sermon will tell you how much they appreciated it. It's important to respond correctly to them.

  The key thing to remember is that your grateful listeners are communicating either one or both of the following messages: (1) *I really appreciate the time you took to prepare your sermon, and the courage you summoned up to deliver it;* (2) *Your sermon contained Bible truths that I found important.*

  As you respond to their gratitude, acknowledge *both* messages. It's tempting to quickly say something such as "Praise the Lord. To God be the glory." That recognizes the second message, but not the first. You need to show your personal appreciation for their kind words as well.

Here's how I often combine the two.

Listener: *Pastor, thank you so much for your message. It really spoke to me today.*

Maylan: *You're welcome. Thanks for the encouragement.* (At this point I often hold up my Bible, which I've carried with me from the pulpit.) *I had good material to work with!* (or) *Thank the Lord for giving us His Bible.*

Resist the urge to start talking about how you created the sermon, how long it took you, how you wish you'd had more time. Just say thanks.

Once in a great while someone will take you aside and give you what they think is helpful advice. This happened to me the first day I preached at a church I was serving as assistant pastor. A man came up to me at the door and told me that I had made five grammatical errors in my sermon.

Grammar's important, of course—because bad grammar will definitely distract people from your message. But two things burned me. First, my grammar errors were minor ones, and I was deliberately trying to be colloquial. I think he was being picky. Second, I was stunned that he would gleefully keep count. I mildly said something like "Thanks for listening—and thanks for your input." That's as good a response as any.

Homework Project 12—Preach That Sermon!

GROUP DISCUSSION STARTERS

Note: This is the final set of Group Discussion Starters.

Group members should describe, one by one, how they plan to prepare and use sermon notes in the pulpit. This might be a great time to glean helpful rubber-meets-the-road ideas from one another.

If your group meets in a church, go into the sanctuary and practice with the microphone (if necessary, ask one of the sound system operators to be with you). Each group member should read his or her own Bible preaching passage aloud into the microphone. Other members should fan out in all directions to the most distant places in the sanctuary and listen, then offer suggestions. Pay special attention to (a) speaking directly into the mike, but (b) neither getting too close nor retreating too far. (If an audio person is present, ask him or her for feedback—no, not the *squeal-y* kind!)

As long as you're all in the sanctuary, why not have each group member preach the introduction to his or her sermon? The others could make comments using the "3-1 rule"—three positive comments and one suggestion for improvement.

At the sanctuary entrance, each group member should practice saying thanks when complimented on his or her sermon.

11

"Why We Need Him" General Notes—An Example of How I Create a Sermon From Scratch

I thought it might be useful to you to watch what I do as I create an actual sermon from scratch. At the time I wrote this chapter I was actually starting on a new sermon, and I decided to make my general notes not in my composition book but here on the computer screen, and let you watch me do it. This chapter will be my general notes, and chapter 12 will contain the actual sermon I preached.

So here goes.

Right now, as I'm writing this, I don't know what the sermon will be about. But by the end of this chapter I'll have found out—and so will you! (Incidentally, to make it easier I'm using voice recognition software. I'm speaking into a headset, and as I do so, the words are appearing on the screen in front of me. It's a weird feeling, because I've never taken general notes like this before. And I'll probably never do it again, because I think better with my fingers on a keyboard, or holding a pen!)

This sermon will be the first in a miniseries. It's late November, and I need four sermons to bring me up to Christmas. So I thought I would look back at some of the messianic passages in the Old Testament, pick four of them, and create an expository sermon on each. I'm considering calling the series "Why We Need Him." Each of the sermons will answer the question "Why do my listeners and I desperately need Jesus, the Son of God?"

I think I'll start with Genesis 3, because as far as I can tell, this chapter contains the Bible's first prediction of Jesus the Messiah ("He shall bruise your head, and you shall bruise His heel" [verse 15]).

The first thing I do, as I mentioned earlier in the book, is to print out a copy of the chapter, using my Bible software. Before I had Bible software I would photocopy the chapter from the Bible itself—often cutting it into individual columns—and put each column on a blank white piece of paper. This would leave a lot of white space, in case I'd want to take notes there. But as I say, all my notes are going directly onto my laptop screen, right here.

And not only have I made no previous notes on this chapter, I am not drawing from other sermons I've preached on this topic. I'm starting fresh, and you'll know about my ideas as soon as I will. I will not consult commentaries or even Bible dictionaries during this time.

The way I've printed it off, Genesis 3 takes two pages. I have laid the pages side by side just in front of my keyboard, and am now reading through them. (I'd suggest that you open your Bible to this chapter as well, and read it through before continuing.) To me, what I'm doing right now is really the most exciting part of creating a sermon, because I know that somewhere in those verses is a pattern, and it's up to me—with the guidance of the Holy Spirit—to find it.

So now I'll pray:

Dear Lord, as I begin working on this sermon, please help me to find within this chapter what You would like my congregation to hear. If I'm supposed to choose another chapter, or take a different direction, please guide me. Thank You for the privilege of preaching Your Word. In Jesus' name, amen.

General Notes on Genesis 3

As I read through this chapter, I remember an interesting comment someone made about the Bible. "The first two chapters of the Bible [Genesis 1 and 2] talk about God's perfect world that once was," this person said. "The last two chapters of the Bible [Revelation 21 and 22] talk about God's perfect world that will be restored. The third chapter from the front [Genesis 3] tells how sin entered God's perfect world, and the third chapter from the end [Revelation 20] shows how sin will be destroyed forever. The rest of the Bible in between tells the story of how God reached out to humanity to redeem us through His divine Son, Jesus."

At this point I don't know whether I'll use that comment in my sermon, but I note it down. Now I'm going to read through Genesis 3 again. As I do so, I'll keep in mind my series title: "Why We Need Him."

We have an adversary.

At first glance it seems to me that the main reason we need Jesus is that we have an extremely seductive adversary, Satan the devil. (Revelation 12:9 tells us that one of the devil's names was indeed "that old serpent" [KJV]). I mean, here were Adam and Eve, fresh and perfect from the hand of God. They were not sinners. Sin had not been programmed into them. You and I are weak—they were strong. Innocent, but strong.

Yet Satan—speaking through the serpent—was able to seduce Eve into distrusting God. OK, that could be one of our first points. "We need Him—Jesus—because Satan tempts us to distrust God." (I recognize that this isn't a definite point yet. As I mentioned in chapter 4, the first few notes I make may not be very useful, except to guide me to something that *is* useful.)

But the fact that we have an adversary is an important point nonetheless. Sin isn't merely a philosophical debate—with God's ideas being right and other ideas being wrong. *A deceiver, a fallen angel, has deliberately set out to sabotage God's creation.*

Hey, I just thought of an illustration! (That happy event, an illustration that pops into my head and exactly fits what I need, happens once in a while—especially if I'm not working under a deadline.)

Here's the illustration: Downstairs in our kitchen is a box of cereal produced by a company that donates 10 percent of its profits to peace. But when I go to that company's Web site, they mention nothing about Jesus Christ, the *Prince* of Peace. Instead, they urge you to try to come to peace with yourself through meditation and mantras. They're missing the point! (But in my sermon I will *not* mention the cereal's brand name.)

I'm tempted to spend some sermon time actually talking about just *how* Satan deceived Eve. First, he directly accused God of lying (Gen. 3:4). Second, he charged God with selfishness—withholding something desirable from Eve and her husband (verse 5). Third, he slyly fell silent, knowing Eve's psychology and how God gave her not only a mind, but the ability to process ideas for herself.

The problem was, of course, that Eve's reasoning needed to start in the right place: with God's statements accepted as true. Yet rather than remembering His warnings and obeying them without question, Eve instead began to study the forbidden tree and its fruit, using human logic, rather than the divine command, to evaluate it.

There, a couple of paragraphs up—when I was talking about how Satan deceived Eve—we already have a potential three-point sermon. (I even included a "first," "second," and "third.") But I'm not going to follow that plan quite yet, because I haven't read the whole chapter.

Adam and Eve ate the fruit, suddenly discovered that they were naked, and tried to cover themselves. And as evening fell, they heard God walking in the garden. Another line of thought suddenly springs to my mind. When Satan entered the garden, he immediately introduced conflict and doubt. When God came to the garden, He was simply calling for companionship: "Adam, Eve, where are you?"

Satan desires discord; God wants friendship.

Again, that too is an interesting line of thought—though not quite as crisp as my three-point mini-sermon outline a few paragraphs back. But I continue to study the chapter and make notes.

What strikes me next is the amazing way God spoke to Adam and Eve. Obviously, He knew very well what they had done. But rather than approach them angrily, read them the charges, and punish them, God asked questions. To me, this shows a deity who doesn't simply require obedience, but who seeks understanding from us as well.

Now, *that* might be the line to take. Here's a God I could be comfortable with—a God who is totally unlike the deity you often see pictured in cartoons: the white-haired cranky old man in a long white robe standing on a cloud and flinging lightning bolts. Here is a God who approaches gently, almost humbly, asking careful questions.

And God surprises us further by allowing Adam and Eve to guide the conversation. "Have you eaten from the tree?" He asked. Adam answered, "The woman made me do it!"

"Is that right?" God said thoughtfully, and turned to the woman. "Well, what did you do?"

Eve pointed to the snake and said, "The snake made me do it!"

Now at any point in this rather silly conversation God could have held up His hands. "Hold it," He could have said. "Enough of this nonsense. You are all responsible for your own acts."

But He didn't say that. I mean, God must have been feeling terrible. Rather than a joyous eternity in this garden with His precious children, He faced the agony of watching as murder and death and sickness rot and corrode the bodies and minds of their descendants. *Yet God did not allow His feelings to run away with Him. Instead, He treated Adam and Eve the way a wise mother or father might deal with their children when they've done something naughty.*

OK. If God is the parent here, what role is Satan playing? The bully? The persecutor? (That would be great alliteration, wouldn't it? Parent versus Persecutor!) It's interesting, isn't it, that when God came on the scene, the snake stopped talking. Remember how during Jesus' ministry the demons instantly became cowards?

Again, all sorts of ideas here. But I'm not done reading the chapter. Let's keep going. What about those "curses"? Why would God level curses against the three other characters of the story? It seems such an un-twenty-first-century thing to do. Yet that is what God did. And this is an important point to remember as you read through the Bible chapters you choose for your sermons: *Don't second-guess God.* If God *says* something, and if God *does* something, He has good reasons. We may not understand what they are right now, but those reasons are still good.

At this point I remember another illustration that I have found helpful. I have already used this in a sermon not too long ago, so you're welcome to it if it would work for you.

Let's pretend that time travel is really possible. And let's imagine that Benjamin Franklin, wise old scientist and inventor, suddenly finds himself time-transported into my home office. There he stands, blinking cautiously through his granny glasses, staring around the room. He sees the blaze of light coming from my floor lamp—far brighter than any candle or oil lamp he has ever seen. A silver electric fan sits on top of my bookcase, but since he has never seen a fan and doesn't realize that the electricity he toyed with while kite flying could ever spin a motor, he doesn't know what the fan is. Maybe he thinks it's a metal sculpture of a flower.

I hand him my cordless phone. He turns it over and over in his hand courteously, and gives me a questioning glance. I push a few buttons and hand it back to him, adjusting it to his ear. He listens for a second; then his knees weaken, and he collapses on the floor.

"Witchcraft!" he screams. "May the heavenly saints protect us! I heard a spirit voice in my ear!"

I stare at him and suddenly decide not to point out the digital clock hanging on the wall. And unless I want to send him directly to a mental institution, I'm *certainly* not going to show him my computer!

The point I make when I use that illustration is that God knows so much more than we do that it is foolish even to try to second-guess Him. Make no mistake—God loves to reason with us, loves it when we ask Him questions, and has absolutely no problem with our at first disagreeing with some of His ideas as long as we are willing to keep an open mind and allow Him to continue teaching us. Think of all the psalms that begin with agonized cries of temporary doubt and fear and confusion, but conclude with faith.

But just as Benjamin Franklin could not possibly understand the electronic gadgets in my office until he received some long and careful orientation, in the same way it might be necessary for me simply to trust God about puzzles I don't yet understand.

OK. Let's send Ben Franklin back to the 1700s and continue with Genesis 3. God pronounced the curses, starting with the snake and then moving on to Adam and Eve. Again, why would God deliberately make things more difficult for them? You can understand His cursing the serpent, but why inflict thorns and thistles and sweat on Adam, and labor pains on Eve?

At this point, if I weren't as experienced as I am, I might consider the above question an interesting rabbit trail to follow. True, there must be an answer to that question, but is it of sufficient value to spend 30 minutes on this coming weekend? Probably not. Especially since the chapter contains so many other intriguing possibilities.

At this point I realize that, since it's Tuesday of Thanksgiving week and since my brother and his family are coming to visit on Thursday, I had better decide what to do about my SPICAT outline. So I go back to the chapter and read it carefully through again. I can't emphasize enough how important it is to keep going back through your chapter. Read it in different translations—mainly the literal ones, although a quick dip into *The Message* can be exhilarating. Say your passage out loud. Get someone *else* to read it out loud to you. If you have the Bible on tape or CD, play it and listen to it.

Now that I've read the chapter through again, it seems to me that I do need to focus on the devil as the reason we need Jesus. Again, sin is not simply bad thinking. Sin began in the mind of an angel who chose to distrust God and tempt others to do so. When God confronted Adam and Eve with their sin, He didn't simply let the snake slither away into the grass. It had to stay right there and receive the first curse. The snake—in other words, the devil speaking through the snake—is the one whom Jesus will eventually destroy.

OK. How shall I set this up? The sermon series topic is "Why We Need Him." Let's tackle the approach sentence.

Possible approach sentence: *Genesis 3 gives us several reasons we need Jesus.*

Is that a good one? Can it be made better? At least it's down on paper (or laptop screen). We've captured it, and if we get it down, we have something to work with.

Now for the sermon points themselves. Maybe we *should* go back to that three-point sermon I discovered—the three ways Satan deceived Eve.

We can make them more general. Let's try it out and see how it works.

Point 1: *Satan tempts us to believe that God is a liar.*

Point 2: *Satan tempts us to believe that God is selfish.*

Point 3: *Satan tempts us to believe that God's commands aren't necessary.*

So far so good. On the plus side, the points are fairly parallel. Each begins with "Satan tempts us to believe that—" On the minus side, the parallelism stops after the word "God." "Liar" is a noun. "Selfish" is an adjective. "Commands aren't necessary" is actually a mini-sentence (a clause, if you remember your grammar). I'm not saying that you should obsess about parallelism as some people do about alliteration, but—

Wait. I just thought of a better point 3:

Point 3: *Satan tempts us to believe that God isn't necessary.*

I like that better, because it's shorter and has more punch to it. After all, wasn't that what Satan was tempting Eve to believe? Once he'd planted his "God's a liar, God's selfish" ideas in her mind, he shut his mouth and let her wrestle with them, *using her human wisdom.* And to the devil's absolute delight, Eve chose to distrust God.

All right. This seems like a workable outline. Let's look at these points again.

Point 1: *Satan tempts us to believe that God is a liar.*

Point 2: *Satan tempts us to believe that God is selfish.*

Point 3: *Satan tempts us to believe that God simply isn't necessary.*

Whoops! One more revision to point 3, which I thought of a few minutes later.

Point 1: *Satan tempts us to believe that God is a liar.*

Point 2: *Satan tempts us to believe that God is selfish.*

Point 3: *Satan tempts us to believe that God is irrelevant.*

Aha. There we are. It's parallel now, pretty much. I like that.

But wait. (I'm writing this current paragraph a couple days later. Something started bothering me, and I finally realized what it was. Those three points talk about nothing but Satan and his lies. People need to hear about Jesus' response, too. So let's make some additions. How about this?)

Point 1: *Satan claims that God is a liar—but Jesus proves him wrong.*

Point 2: *Satan claims that God is selfish—but Jesus proves him wrong.*

Point 3: *Satan claims that God is irrelevant—but Jesus proves him wrong.*

That's better. It signals to my congregation (and to me as I prepare the sermon) that I'll be talking not just about Satan's lies but how Jesus destroys them.

Now let's go back and make a new approach sentence. This is only temporary, because we haven't chosen the sermon's introduction yet, nor the transition, and the approach is going to have to flow smoothly from both of them. But let's have a shot at it:

Possible approach sentence: Why do we need Him? Genesis 3 tells us we need Jesus because the devil has slandered God in three horrific ways.

Do you see the word "horrific"? I don't normally use a lot of big words in my sermons, but "horrific" seemed to fit right there—after all, the word *sounds* horrifying! I've got to be careful, though, because that's a word I have a habit of using too much. But I don't think I've used it recently.

A few years ago a man came up to me after one of my sermons, grinned, and told me that I used the word "earnest" in every sermon I preached, and that one of his hobbies was counting how often I employed it in a single sermon. Evidently that day I had set a record! I chuckled along with my friend, but his good-humored comments helped me get a grip on that distracting mannerism. (By the way, if your spouse gives you advice about your sermons, listen carefully, and do what he or she says. Back in my early ministry, if I'd been bullheaded and refused to listen to Shelley's suggestions, I wouldn't be writing this book. Maybe I wouldn't even be preaching.)

Now that I have my approach and my points (and all of this is subject to change if a better idea strikes me), my next step will be to go to the illustration file I described in chapter 3 and find four illustrations: one to begin the sermon, and one for each of the SPICATs that I'll be developing from the points.

Another thing I'll be doing right away is going back to Genesis 3 and reading it again, so that I can get to work on the application segment of each SPICAT. In recent years I've put more and more time into the applications, which answer such questions as: "So what? Why is this sermon point important to me? How can I put it to work Monday morning—or in the car on the way home from church today? What difference will this make in my life? How does it affect my view of God? How does it affect my salvation?"

I would say that during the past few years my application segments have grown larger and my comment sections have gotten smaller, which I think is a good thing.

(At this point my deadline was getting close, so I stopped dictating this chapter and got to work on the sermon directly. And in the next chapter you'll read the entire message.)

I hope this has given you a helpful glimpse of what I go through pretty much every week. It's not really any easier than when I began preaching, but it's tremendously satisfying. I believe it's what God called me to do.

And if you've made it this far through this book, maybe lay preaching is what God is urging you to do as well. May He sustain, encourage, and bless you as you seek His will for your preaching.

12

"Why We Need Him"—The Complete Expository Sermon

Note to readers: What follows this paragraph is the sermon I actually preached based on the general notes I made in chapter 11. If you haven't yet done so, go back and read chapter 11, because it shows you how I developed this sermon. To help you see how it all fits together, I've labeled in **bold type** *all the sermon elements. Naturally, I did* **not** *mention them or call attention to them when I preached the sermon. In other words, I don't solemnly say things like "I will begin with my sermon introduction" or "Here is my illustration." Shelley once gave me a very wise bit of advice. "Don't let them see the skeleton," she said.*

Why We Need Him
Expository Sermon on Genesis 3
by Maylan Schurch

Sermon Introduction

Please open your Bibles to Genesis, chapter 3.

This past spring, as I was going through boxes and barrels as we got our Bothell house ready to sell, I discovered a large manila envelope that said "Perry Clifford" on it.

Back in the late 1920s Perry and Inez Clifford were a farm couple living in Faulk County, right next to Spink County, where I would later grow up. But farming wasn't their passion. True, they owned a farm. True, they worked their fields and planted their crops. But they tended to leave both their planting and their harvesting until it was too late.

This had nothing to do with their work ethic, or their intelligence, or their morality. They weren't depriving their children, because they didn't *have* children. Perry, who had graduated with a degree from South Dakota State University in Brookings, was something of a traveling state milk inspector too, so I guess they were in no danger of starving.

It's just that they had other priorities. Their true passion, which took over every part of their lives, was music. Perry and Inez had met at SDSU, and while there they had had the chance to hear huge choirs sing—not only the student choir, but also large choral groups from Minneapolis and other cities.

And the sound of those refined, mellow voices echoing through the auditorium set their blood racing. I don't know how many times they sat side by side at those concerts, holding hands, tears streaming down their faces. But I do know that once their college days were behind them and their farming days ahead, they began to dream. And dream big.

The Cliffords were one of those rare couples who match huge dreams with huge stubbornness—a fierce refusal to let discouragement stop them. As they farmed their acreage on those flat, weary prairies, they were not content to attend church socials and dazzle everybody by reminiscing about the choirs they'd heard.

No, their dream was to gather farmers and their wives from all over Faulk County and train them to sing. Not just to sing four-part hymnal harmony for Sunday services, but to present a concert of as much of Handel's *Messiah* as they could possibly swallow and hold inside.

What followed was a magnificent example of how creative you can get if you will simply allow yourself to be ruled by your dreams. Normally *Messiah* is sung at Christmas. But that schedule had to be discarded. Because it takes months and months of rehearsal to get "Surely He Hath Borne Our Griefs" and "The Glory of the Lord," and even the "Hallelujah Chorus" thoroughly injected into the pioneer bloodstream. And months and months is what farmers *don't* have when they might still be harvesting into early October.

So Perry and Inez decided that *Messiah* would have to be performed at Easter, and that the rehearsals would happen during the winter. And rather than having everybody drive long distances to group rehearsals—because that might have cut down on the number of singers—the Cliffords decided to toss their snow shovel into the back of their Model T and chug from town to town and church to church to practice with five and six singers at a time.

Can you imagine, if you were Perry and Inez, pulling up in the snow outside a tiny church in the dead of winter, and entering and finding four or five very eager but very untrained singers? Can you imagine singing them through their parts, again and again and again, polishing off the rough edges? Can you imagine doing that two nights later with another handful of farmers in the next town over? And can you imagine bringing the entire group together in early April for just a few full rehearsals?

But that's what Inez and Perry did for three decades, starting in 1927. That's when they founded the Faulk County Chorus, which for 30 years sang not only *Messiah* but operettas and all other kinds of music. Eventually the chorus traveled to Detroit to take part in a national choral festival. Among their singers were my mother's cousin Ervin Anderson and my grandfather Cyrus Pettigrew.

Years later, when anyone would mention the Cliffords in their presence, both men's eyes would mist over. An almost worshipful look would come over their faces, and they would begin to tell stories of those rehearsals and concerts, and how dreary the prairie would have seemed if it hadn't been for Perry and Inez and their never-say-die determination.

Transition

It's no secret that we're entering the season that is at least partly devoted to Someone else with a dream, Someone with a determination to enter our sin-twisted planet and, against all odds, teach us to sing a more hopeful song.

What I'd like to do, for the four weeks leading up to Christmas, is to go back into the Old Testament and find some of the prophecies of the Messiah, and discover why those prophecies meant so much to the people God sent them to—why they needed Him. And I believe that we'll find that the reasons that they needed the Messiah were the ones that *we* need Him too.

As far as I can tell, Genesis 3 is the Bible's first prophecy of the Messiah—verse 15, which says that one of the offspring of Eve would finally bruise Satan the serpent's head.

And the Genesis 3 reason that Adam and Eve and the rest of us needed Jesus is that there is a devil. Because sin isn't just bad thinking or leaky philosophy. Sin is a sneery, gut-level rebellion against God, a rebellion that first sprouted and grew in the heart of a talented angel.

Approach (a paragraph rather than a sentence, in this instance; I've bolded the key word)

As Genesis 3 begins, we learn three shameful **lies** that Satan told Eve about God. But as the chapter—and the rest of the Bible—go along, Jesus proves that each of those lies is wrong. And that's why we need Him so much. Let me show you what I mean.

SPICAT 1

- *Scripture: Genesis 3:1-4:* "Now the serpent was more cunning than any beast of the field which the Lord God had made. And he said to the woman, 'Has God indeed said, "You shall not eat of every tree of the garden"?' And the woman said to the serpent, 'We may eat the fruit of the trees of the garden; but of the fruit of the tree which is in the midst of the garden, God has said, "You shall not eat it, nor shall you touch it, lest you die."' Then the serpent said to the woman, 'You will not surely die.'"
- *Point: Why do we need Jesus? Because Satan claims that God is a liar.*
- *Illustration: [This Bible chapter contains a story, so the illustrations can be brief. In fact, illustrations sometimes intrude awkwardly into a Bible story, because they tend to jolt the hearer back into the twenty-first century. If you make sure to keep the Bible story interesting enough, you won't need as many illustrations.]* And the suspicion that God is a liar is dangerous. It's like suspecting that your *doctor* is a liar. That could be dangerous to your health, and dangerous to the doctor's reputation.
- *Comment:* Eve knew that God had created her. She had probably many conversations with Him since He first brought her to life. She knew the sound of His voice. She had assumed—up to now—that God had always been telling her the truth, including the part about how she was not to eat from the tree of the knowledge of good and evil.

In all her young life Eve has never heard a lie. So now, as she listens to the devil speaking through his snakish ventriloquist dummy, she is quite confused. Suddenly, for the very first time, she is forced to choose between two firmly stated ideas that are in total disagreement with each other. God had said, "The very day you eat from the tree, you're going to die." And now the snake says, "You will *not* die."

As you know, the "God is a liar" idea is getting a lot of publicity these days. Evolutionists claim that the Bible creation story is a myth. And a casual stroll through Borders or Barnes and Noble will introduce you to hundreds and thousands of other voices who call God a liar.

You'll see books of philosophy in which God is either ignored or jeered at. You'll see pagan magazines that preach that a godless magic is available to everybody. You can stroll over to the oldies section of the music area and put on headphones and hear John Lennon singing

"Imagine," in which he wistfully dreams of a peaceful world while ignoring the only One who can cause it to happen. "Imagine there's no heaven," he sings. "It's easy if you try."

And even the entertainment business is calling God a liar. Glance at any movie marquee, and you will see the names of films that systematically glorify the sins that the Ten Commandments warn against—murder, adultery, theft, lying, coveting, disobeying parents, taking God's name in vain. All the superhero movies subtly teach hero worship or even self-worship rather than God worship. (Did you ever see Superman or Batman or Spiderman or the Incredible Hulk praying to God for help?)

"God is a liar, Eve," Satan hissed. She stared solemnly at him as she digested that idea. And as she digested it, the poison entered her bloodstream.

But just when we needed Him, Jesus came to prove the devil wrong. How did He do this? One way He did it was to go right to work, all through the Old Testament and then in the New Testament, to prove that God tells the truth. Many Bible scholars believe that whenever God interacted with people in the Old Testament, He did it through Jesus.

That means that since John 1:18 says that "no one has seen God at any time" it must have been *Jesus* who approached the tent of Abraham and told him about the birth of his son Isaac, and then about the destruction of Sodom and Gomorrah. Those things happened—God tells the truth. It must have been Jesus who wrestled with Jacob at night, assuring him that God was no fickle deity whose story changed from moment to moment, but who *kept* covenants with people.

And Jesus appeared with three brave Hebrew young men in the center of a blazing furnace to demonstrate, again, that when God says He can protect, He really can.

And then, of course, Jesus came as a real human being to show us what kind of smile God smiled, what kind of voice tones He used, what kind of power He had. *Satan* was using whatever methods he could to spread *lies* about God—and about Jesus Himself—but Jesus proved that our God of love is not a liar. "I and My Father are one," He told us in John 10:30, and in another book written by John, in Revelation 3:14, Jesus calls Himself "faithful and true" (KJV).

- *Application:* So now that I've seen Jesus suffocate Satan's lie and remind me that God is truthful, what should I do?

What I need to do is to let a deeper respect for the Bible grow within me. "All Scripture . . . is profitable . . . for instruction," Paul said in

2 Timothy 3:16, so I should bathe my mind in the Bible's pages at least as much as I bathe it in any other kind of literature or TV program or whatever. That's the best possible way to block the devil's lies from having an effect on me.

A new year is coming up—and right now would be a great time to choose a Bible version to read through this coming year. Our church Web site has a daily Bible reading guide, and if you'd like some other options, just talk to me after the service or e-mail me.

- **Transition:** Now back to Genesis 3. As he chats with Eve, Satan isn't satisfied merely to claim that God is a liar. Notice what he does next.

SPICAT 2

- **Scripture: Verses 4, 5:** "Then the serpent said to the woman, 'You will not surely die. For God knows that in the day you eat of it your eyes will be opened.'"
- **Point:** *Why do we need Jesus? Because Satan not only claims that God is a liar, but also claims that God is selfish.*
- **Illustration from the Bible story:** *[This SPICAT actually has two illustrations. The first comes directly from the Genesis 3 story, and the second—which I mention later—is from contemporary life.]* Notice what Satan was claiming here. He told Eve that when she ate the forbidden fruit, her eyes would be opened. As Eve stood there staring at the snake, she may have thought to herself:

Wait a minute. My eyes are open. I can see the garden. I can see the tree. I can see this snake. But this snake says that my eyes aren't really open. So there must be a kind of vision I don't have now that I will have when I eat this fruit.

But if in some way my eyes are still shut, that must mean that God has been holding something back from me. I didn't suspect before that God could be selfish, but this talking snake is hinting that He is. The snake says that God knows that my eyes will be opened when I eat this fruit. I've never heard a talking snake before—but this one must have had his eyes opened, to make him so intelligent and articulate. And if this fruit can make a snake talk, what amazing things will it do for a human being who can already talk?

- **Comment:** The "God is selfish" idea, like the "God is a liar" idea, is also getting a lot of play these days.

[Illustration from contemporary life:] Last March I heard about a restaurant in Zurich, Switzerland, called The Blind Cow. It has been designed to give sighted people a chance to discover what it's like to be in a

restaurant and be totally blind. At the door a waiter asks you for your coat and any light-producing devices such as a luminous watch. And then you are ushered into a totally dark room.

All around, you can hear people talking and silverware clinking. There is no background music, so you can hear people all the way across the room. Soon you hear a voice—your waiter has arrived. All the waiters are either totally blind or have limited sight. You place your order, and soon your food arrives. And if you're not used to eating in the dark, you have to make some adjustments.

[Comment continues:] Once she'd listened to Satan, I wonder if Eve felt that somehow, even after eating all the other kinds of fruit from all the other trees in the garden, she was still eating in a Blind Cow restaurant. *I wonder, she may have thought to herself, what it would be like to have my eyes opened the way this serpent's were.*

I looked up the word "enlightenment" in my *American Heritage Dictionary*. Its first definition was "the act or means of enlightening." The second definition was "the state of being enlightened."

But its third definition was: ***"Enlightenment:*** A philosophical movement of the eighteenth century that emphasized the use of reason to scrutinize previously accepted doctrines and traditions . . ."

Now, if you know your history, you know that the Enlightenment did do a lot of good. When you rip away the curtains of false and harmful doctrines and traditions and beliefs, then the truth can shine through. People get healthier. They live longer. They are less superstitious. They can make better sense of the real world.

But some of the Enlightenment thinkers also decided that you should ignore the Bible and figure things out for yourself, using your own mind. It's no secret that the Christian church hasn't always been free from false ideas. And since the church claimed to speak for God, it was easy for the Enlightenment philosophers to say, "The idea of God Himself must also be anti-reason. Why should we listen to what He says, since His representatives seem so selfish and so mulishly backward in their thinking?"

The idea that God is selfish is another lie Jesus came to obliterate.

- *Application:* Is God selfish? Look at Jesus hanging on the cross, and His whole life of unselfish service, and the devil has no justification for his lie.

[Note to readers: One of the lay preachers who evaluated this manuscript told

me that I should have developed that application more. He said, "If a fussing baby distracted a listener, he or she might miss this vital point." He's right, of course.]

- **Transition:** So far we've watched Jesus explode two of the devil's lies—that God is a liar and that God is selfish. But Satan is about to introduce us to his third and most horrific—and most effective—lie.

SPICAT 3

- **Scripture: Verses 4, 5:** "Then the serpent said to the woman, 'You will not surely die. For God knows that in the day you eat of it your eyes will be opened, and you will be like God, knowing good and evil.'"
- **Point:** *Why do we need Jesus? Because Satan claims not only that God is a liar, and that God is selfish, but also that God is irrelevant.*
- **Illustration:** In other words, the devil says that we can become *like* God. And therefore, God is no longer needed. God is superfluous. God is dispensable, discardable.

In our kitchen cupboard down in Renton we have a couple boxes of a cereal that is very healthful and good-tasting. This company not only makes nutritious cereal, but devotes a percentage of their profits to peace, and gives monetary grants to organizations they think are working for global harmony.

That's a very worthy cause, and I'm sure they are doing what seems best to them. But as I glanced over their Web site, I noticed that there was no reference at all to the *Prince* of Peace. I clicked on their Inner Peace link, and it took me to a screen that said I could have inner peace if I chanted mantras and did other mystic exercises.

All of which is very interesting. But no matter where I went on that Web site, I could find no reference to Jesus, the Prince of Peace. These well-meaning cereal creators have lofty goals and they do a lot of good, but to them, God is irrelevant.

- **Comment:** "God is *certainly* irrelevant," the devil agrees. "In fact, I don't even care whether you believe that God is a liar or selfish, just as long as you decide He's irrelevant."

Is God irrelevant? Watch Him as He responds to the entrance of sin into His beautiful garden.

Verses 6-9: "So when the woman saw that the tree was good for food, that it was pleasant to the eyes, and a tree desirable to make one wise, she took of its fruit and ate. She also gave to her husband with her, and he ate. Then the eyes of both of them were opened, and they knew that they were naked; and they sewed fig leaves together and made themselves coverings. And they heard the sound of the Lord God walking in the garden in the cool of the day, and Adam and his wife hid themselves from the presence of the Lord God among the trees of the garden. Then the Lord God called to Adam and said to him, 'Where are you?'"

Is God irrelevant? He could have *made* Himself irrelevant if He'd wanted to. He could have walked *away from* His children that evening, rather than toward them. My Hubble space telescope coffee table book at home shows me that there are thousands and thousands and thousands of other galaxies about the size of the Milky Way. He could have gone and visited them, and just left Adam and Eve alone.

The question isn't so much "Is God relevant to me?" as it is "Am I relevant to God?" And of course I am. Of course we are. Notice how gently and carefully our brokenhearted God deals with His children.

Verses 9-13: "Then the Lord God called to Adam and said to him, 'Where are you?' So he said, 'I heard Your voice in the garden, and I was afraid because I was naked; and I hid myself.' And He said, 'Who told you that you were naked? Have you eaten from the tree of which I commanded you that you should not eat?' Then the man said, 'The woman whom You gave to be with me, she gave me of the tree, and I ate.' And the Lord God said to the woman, 'What is this you have done?' The woman said, 'The serpent deceived me, and I ate.'"

And what is so awesome is that at any moment the Lord could have stopped that foolish chatter. "Enough of that," He could have said. "Quit playing the blame game. You have free choice. You're responsible for your *own* sins."

But instead He gentles them along. He lets them lead the conversation. He tells them matter-of-factly some of the results of their terrible choice. But as He does so, He introduces "Exhibit A evidence" that He and we are relevant to each other.

Verses 13-15: "And the Lord God said to the woman, 'What is this you have done?' The woman said, 'The serpent deceived me, and I ate.' So the Lord God said to the serpent: 'Because you have done this, you are cursed more than all cattle, and more than every beast of the field; on your belly you shall go, and you shall eat dust all the days of your life. And I will put enmity between you and the woman, and between your seed and her Seed; He shall bruise your head, and you shall bruise His heel.'"

- *Application*: Why do we need Jesus? Because He needs us. He loves us. He needs us and loves us so much that He finally came to die for us. We deserve death. The very day that Adam and Eve ate from the fruit, they did die—through the death of the animals that were sacrificed to give them skins to wear, which symbolized the death their Creator would eventually die for them.

[*The same lay preacher/evaluator who commented a few paragraphs back had an observation again at this point: "Jesus' relevance needs to be given more time. Look at how a godless world lives—wars, loneliness, depression—compared with the fullness of joy that He'd like us to have." Again, he's probably right. It's possible that I was trying to cover too much important material in this sermon.*]

Sermon Conclusion/Appeal (beginning, in this case, with a tie-in to my opening illustration)

If you've heard my Clifford story before, you may remember how it ends. Perry and Inez retired and moved to the same town where I was attending college. I would visit them once a week and play chess with Perry. That's when he gave me what was in the manila envelope—a lot of Faulk County Chorus memorabilia.

After I graduated I went down to Lincoln, Nebraska, to teach. I heard that they had both entered a nursing home in Faulkton, the Faulk County seat.

And then Perry died. Inez raved with incoherent grief for two weeks before she too died. Why? Because they needed each other. They couldn't live apart from each other.

If you died apart from God, God would grieve. And He would grieve not with puny human grief, but great, sobbing heavenly cries. "How can I give you up?" He would cry. "How can I let you go?"

Let's not put Him through that, OK? Let's recognize how much we need Him, and His Son, and His Holy Spirit.

Let's assure Him that we know He's truthful, self-sacrificing, and desperately relevant to our day-to-day lives. And let's cling so closely to Him that when He appears in the sky above us, we can take our first electric, immortal breath and shout a greeting to our King of glory.

APPENDIX

Some Resources I've Found Helpful

Resources I Use While Working on a Sermon
This brief list consists of resources that I employ constantly.

Logos Bible Software (Libronix Digital Library System). Several good Bible software programs are available—this just happens to be the one I use. *Important:* Even though it has a lot of helpful commentary-style information on it, I employ it for only four reasons: to be able to see more than one Bible version side by side; to cut and paste chapters into my word processor so that I can print them out and carry them around with me; to do concordance-like word searches; and to look verses up quickly. You'll find this and other good Bible software at your Christian bookstore.

Parallel Bibles. Two books I highly recommend place a total of 16 Bible versions side by side: *The Precise Parallel New Testament* (Oxford University Press, 1995) and *The Evangelical Parallel New Testament* (Oxford University Press, 2003).

Thompson Chain Reference Bible in a version of your choice. (See chapter 3 for a description and discussion.)

The NIV Study Bible (see chapter 3).

Strong's Concordance. If you're fairly familiar with the King James Version or New King James Version, you'll find *Strong's* helpful, especially if you don't have Bible software. I use it for looking up the location of a text I half remember. A tip: get the Comfort Print edition.

American Heritage Dictionary (latest edition). This dictionary will not only build your biceps; it's really something of a mini-encyclopedia. A "hugely" valuable book!

The Synonym Finder, by J. I. Rodale. I have several more recent thesauruses, but this one's still the quickest way—containing the most options—for a busy preacher to find a synonym.

International Standard Bible Encyclopedia. I talk about this in chapter 3. If you buy this four-volume set, you will own a huge treasury of dependable Bible information.

Eerdmans Dictionary of the Bible. A one-volume Bible dictionary more up-to-date than the ISBE above.

Google.com. Good old Google—what would we do without it? *However,* remember that not everything you read online is true. I use Google for everything from getting some background on a historical figure to finding song lyrics or poetry I want to quote. And I will most often double-check other sites to make sure that the information is accurate.

Other Good Resources

Bartlett's Familiar Quotations. Get the latest edition, and then nose around in a used bookstore for a much earlier one.

Two or three recent slang dictionaries. Yes, the ones with the dirty words. Every once in a while, if I suspect I'm innocently using a word that has become obscene, I'll grab one of these dictionaries and check it out. I don't want to send teenagers (or anyone else) into muffled giggles and have them miss the sermon's important points.

Preaching God's Word: A Hands-on Approach to Preparing, Developing, and Delivering the Sermon, by Terry G. Carter, J. Scott Duvall, and J. Daniel Hays (Zondervan, 2005). I flipped through this in a bookstore a couple weeks ago, and it seems to be a very good contemporary discussion of preaching for beginning students.

World Almanac (latest edition). I get a new one every year. An inexpensive way to keep current on important world facts.

Dragon NaturallySpeaking Voice-Recognition Software (latest version). I have Version 8, which eliminated some bugs from Version 7, and is even more accurate than before. A great help for answering e-mail too.

Sermon Evaluation Form

(See Homework Project 1 [chapter 1])

Directions: Use a copier to enlarge this form to 8.5" x 11". **Then fold the bottom half underneath so you can't see it,** and fill out *only* the top half during the sermon itself. The next day, complete the bottom half.

Speaker's Name _____ Date _____

Sermon Title _____ Main Bible Text _____

Fill out this first section while you're listening to the sermon. After reading each question, CIRCLE the response you most agree with. DO NOT READ OR FILL OUT the part below the dotted line until the day after the sermon.

1. Could you easily understand the speaker? **yes   no**
2. If **no,** was it the speaker's fault or the sound system's fault?
   speaker   sound system
3. The speaker spoke: **too quickly   about right   too slowly**
4. Did the speaker read aloud from a real Bible during the sermon?
   yes   no
5. If **yes,** approximately how many times? **1 time   2–5 times   more**
6. How did the speaker try to catch and hold the hearers' attention?
   story   startling quote   question   other _____
7. The speaker's gestures and body language were (circle one)
   effective   OK   distracting   nonexistent
8. When the speaker told stories, were they old or more recent?
   old   recent   a combination
9. Did you mostly agree with how the speaker interpreted the Bible?
   yes   no
10. List three things the speaker did effectively.

   a. _____

   b. _____

   c. _____

11. List three things you would have done differently if you had been preaching the sermon.

a. _____

b. _____

c. _____

12. About how long did the sermon last?

20 minutes or under   21-30 minutes   31-45 minutes or longer

FOLD EVERYTHING BELOW THIS DOTTED LINE UNDERNEATH SO YOU CAN'T SEE IT. DON'T LOOK AT IT UNTIL TOMORROW. THEN FILL IT OUT AS BEST YOU CAN.

- -

ANSWER THE FOLLOWING QUESTIONS ON THE DAY AFTER YOU HEARD THE SERMON.

1. In one sentence, describe what the sermon was about.

_____

_____

2. In one sentence, describe one thing the speaker suggested you do as a result of the sermon.

_____

_____

3. Describe the story or illustration you remember most clearly from the sermon.

_____

_____

4. List one or two how-to-preach principles you've learned to use by listening to this sermon.

_____

_____